Cut the Bullsh*t Marketing
A practical guide to creating real impact through marketing

www.cutthebullshitmarketing.com

Copyright © 2017 Sander Arts, Mark Geljon, Jeroen Grit and Robert Slagter

ISBN-13: 978-1546425434
ISBN-10: 1546425438

Visual design by Fenna Klein Tuente

Cut the Bullsh*t Marketing

A practical guide to creating real impact through marketing

By Sander Arts, Mark Geljon, Jeroen Grit
Edited by Robert Slagter

Endorsements

"I am a strong believer in 'applied academic approaches' that take state of the art methodologies and transform this into practical business tools that generate impact. Cut the Bullsh*t Marketing is a great example of 'the best of both worlds' and inspirational for every marketing student."

~ Baba Shiv, Professor of Marketing at Stanford University

"Marketing is only valuable when it leads to more revenue. As described in this book, at Atmel we were able to connect investments in marketing to their bottom line impact. This is what digital marketing provides and is the trend of the future."

~ Steven Laub, Former President and CEO at Atmel Corporation

"My Core belief is that an organization should have "Customer focused; passion to win" at the center of its strategy. At NXP, Sander and his team translated this belief into a marketing approach that generated brand value, increased brand reputation, connected NXP to many new customers, improved NXP's pipeline of projects and increased sales taking NXP from a top 20 player in the semiconductor industry to become one of the top 5. All readers, whether they work in marketing departments or as business leaders will find much to stimulate their thinking in this book. The authors clearly explain why cutting the bullsh*t in marketing reaps benefits for companies. Every marketer should have this philosophy. The book combines storytelling and strong UX approach with practical tools, that will resonate with every professional that wants to create impact."

~ Rick Clemmer, President & CEO at NXP

"Sander, Mark, Jeroen have created a blueprint that every executive should read. Cut the Bullsh*t Marketing proves why it is crucial to understand and reach makers as well as market makers with a personal, engaging experience. With great first hand success stories (such as NXP), they show how to deliver tangible results and meaningful profits. This is a no non-sense, practical book that will impact your business."

~ Mike Noonen, semiconductor executive, founder of Silicon Catalyst, former EVP sales & marketing at NXP

"In private equity, there is no successful investment strategy without improving the operational performance of the assets. Marketing can be a tier 1 operational value driver as the transformation of NXP has shown. This book shares the core mechanics of such excellent marketing at work. It is a great read."

~ Johannes P. Huth, Member of KKR and Head of KKR's operations in EMEA

Foreword

It is a real pleasure for me to write this foreword for my friend and former colleague Sander Arts and his co-authors.

This story goes back to 2004; the year that I joined Philips Semiconductors as CEO. It was the beginning of a great journey. We had the massive task to reposition and grow the company, improve time-to-market, create value through systems solutions, increase customer intimacy and improve the company's profitability. As part of this, we separated the company from Royal Philips and built a new semiconductor brand, NXP. Fueled by these high ambitions, I experienced the benefits of the 'no bullsh*t culture' in the marketing department that is needed to deliver results for customers, employees and shareholders.

Having clear key performance indicators and, most importantly, making our customers the focal point of everything we do with practical application oriented marketing information, were ways of reducing bullsh*t and pivotal to achieving growth. Marketing, by nature, is an area where bullsh*t is more common than, for instance, in Supply Chain or Quality. The models and instruments used in marketing tend to be more qualitative and abstract and marketeers have loads of jargon to tell a story.

How refreshing it was for me to assemble a team of smart yet practical marketeers that really understood that if we wanted to be the best semiconductor manufacturer, we had to remove all the bullsh*t from the way we interacted with our customers and really engage with the engineering audience. The journey we pursued together led to the foundation that made NXP what it is today.

Now, the most impactful learnings are captured in this book. It reflects the essence of what I feel is important when building a company: Engage with your customers and generate revenue and ROI. I believe that anyone involved in B2B or B2C marketing should pick up this book. It will help marketers focus on what matters in large companies, and on what customers truly value. This book will help you become a better professional with a stronger connection into the board room. The authors of this book have proven their impact in Philips and NXP and I have personally seen the strong results of their approach.

Cut the Bullsh*t Marketing covers state-of-the-art marketing techniques that are clear and concise in language and very actionable, without the hyperbole we often see in today's ineffective marketing. The book highlights the importance of clearly identifying and communicating with customers, having a clear, easy-to-understand vision for marketing programs, developing integrated marketing campaigns that include a wide variety of marketing tools and channels and many other topics that will resonate with leaders in marketing. Finally, this is book is all about creating and tracking the right KPIs. Sander, Mark and Jeroen did a great job in bringing this together in a no bullsh*t way, making it a valuable tool for more effectiveness in your daily business.

I am sure this book will give you many great ideas. Hats off to the authors for bringing it to market. Enjoy reading it!

Frans van Houten
CEO Royal Philips
Amsterdam, April 2017

By the authors

"If you decide to be in what is traditionally called business-to-business (B2B) marketing, you'll have to be a bit of a masochist."

This is a quote we use in some of our lectures. Companies, especially those that are in B2B and manufacturing, don't value marketing. Why would you even work for a company like that? Wouldn't it be easier (and more fun) to do consumer marketing?

We have always been attracted to more complex environments and complex products-or commodities, if you like. It is in these environments that we have driven marketing activities. Why? We like the challenge of what sometimes feels like an uphill battle. We love technology and what it can do to make the world a better place. We love the people who work in these companies because they are so tremendously smart. We love environments that aren't very receptive to flashy marketing. We love bringing technology to life.

We also love to be challenged to the maximum! Engineering companies need proof for everything they do. They tend to think in "ones and zeros." Everything needs to be underpinned by data, discussed with reference to data, questioned via data, and justified with data. Every dollar invested in marketing needs to be justified, accounted for. We all know that is hard. But we like it that way.

At a certain point in our careers, we faced even larger challenges: private equity firms. In 2006, a consortium of private equity firms acquired Philips Semiconductors. Philips spun its semiconductor division out of Royal Philips in 2006, and KKR, Bain and Silverlake acquired it, in the biggest leveraged buyout to date at that moment. That created large challenges. Not only did we have to build (and launch!) the NXP brand in less than six weeks, but we also got exposed to the ways of working of private equity firms.

The private equity owners would come in and drive ongoing cost savings, continuously challenging us as to why we are investing the money we are investing. Frankly, in the beginning, it wasn't very encouraging ("Are these guys crazy? Don't they realize they are breaking everything we built?").

Looking back, though, the experience was awesome. It was the best MBA one could take. The beauty of private equity in these environments is that you must prove your existence. Making a nice website, a beautiful piece of text, a logo, a brochure, or a large footprint at a trade show doesn't matter to them. The smartest private equity people and CEOs in the world continuously asked us questions for justification, which meant that we did our best work. It took us a while to step up to the plate, but eventually, we did it. We created marketing campaigns that beat large business-to-consumer (B2C) companies in large award ceremonies. Why? Well, we had results in the form of revenue and increased customer count. Business results! The "shiny object" type of marketing from our competition always lost at those ceremonies from our marketing for impact. Clearly defined markets, personas, targets and business goals combined with great results are hard to beat. We collected many marketing awards across the globe in all kinds of categories (digital, web, brand, public relations, campaigns, etc.). People working for shiny brands in B2C were asking how they could have lost from a small marketing department with no funding in a "boring" B2B environment.

Well, because we were challenged and had to do great work! Every day! The ongoing pressures of cost awareness, being challenged by smart people and needing to show impact forced us to do great work – work that matters, that is without bullsh*t, that has an impact on the brand and on the health of the business, and that (most importantly) ensures that the engineers working for our customers are able to make better designs and build better products. Hence, this work will make a better world!

The ability to step away from the distinction between B2B and B2C and focus on people-to-people marketing through the use of recent technology, thinking and methods created a new paradigm for the marketing of manufacturing companies. This new paradigm could show engagement and contribute to the bottom line of the company.

However, we also see that many marketers create bullsh*t. They pursue shiny objects because they like these objects themselves or because they feel these objects will impress their management. They use bullsh*t and assumptions in their campaign setup, in the choice of marketing channels and in how they sell their marketing within their company. If you are the CEO of a company, and if you are wondering what your marketing department is doing, it is likely that it is wasting your money and delivering bullsh*t work that hasn't been thought through. They don't give you return on investment (ROI) or revenue that you care about. They will tell you it is hard, which it is – but it is also very much doable!

If you are a marketer, and if you are wondering why some heads of marketing make it all the way into the board room as a sparring partner for CEOs, private equity companies, and Boards of Directors, then you have to stop the bullsh*t marketing and embrace the concepts in this book. You must start to deliver and to speak the language of the people who run the business, sell the products, and deliver results that move the needle for the company.

Intrigued? We certainly hope so! Please go and read this book. Marketers, challenge yourselves. Business leaders, start asking for revenue and more customers.

Happy reading.

San Francisco, CA, USA and Utrecht, the Netherlands, Spring 2017

Sander Arts, Mark Geljon, Jeroen Grit

Table of contents

INTRODUCTION

Are you a CEO working with a head of marketing? A private equity firm trying to make sense of a marketing department? Have you also asked yourself what the hell marketing people are doing and if they really contribute? Do you believe they are a cost center and you want them to be a profit center? In that case, you have to read this book. Marketing, if done correctly, is a profit center with lots of ROI, including revenue.

Are you a marketer? Are you struggling to explain to your management why you matter? Do you feel unheard? Do you feel treated like the head of corporate entertainment? Do you feel you continuously have to defend your investments and budget allocation? Do you continuously get hit by budget cuts because you can't show revenue for your investments? Please read this book. It will help you do marketing that matters, marketing that moves the needle. No bullsh*t! Simple, practical cases, easy-to-use models and guidelines, and anecdotes about how we put these to use.

Preface

In recent years, the business world has shifted tremendously: The realization that markets are conversations (Levine et al., 2009) has paved the way for a more personal way of doing business and engaging with customers. As a result, marketing is transforming. Companies explore ways to engage with broader customer groups to reach the long tail in a more personal manner, not just for consumers, but also in business-to-business (B2B) settings. Unfortunately, this transformation has also led a lot of marketers to resort to bullsh*t: creating bullsh*t campaigns, using bullsh*t marketing channels and selling a lot of bullsh*t terminology within the company. Our book presents a way to design and run effective marketing campaigns and engage with your target audience in a personal way to create ROI and revenue without having to resort to bullsh*t.

What do we mean by bullsh*t? By bullsh*t we don't mean models or under-the-hood-plumbing, but rather marketing methods that are sold as off-the-shelf, silver-bullet solutions – marketing advice that oversimplifies a complex landscape or, on the other hand, marketing soluti-ons that are overly complex. In our expe-rience, by acknowledging that the land-scape is complex and putting effort into really understanding the people involved, solutions can be developed that are pragmatic, low cost, and simple. That is what Cut the Bullsh*t Marketing is all about!

In the old days, B2B marketing was aimed at key accounts and focused on reaching the buyers at those accounts, which is an approach that requires more "key account management" than "mass marketing." Therefore, the shift to a more personal approach means a huge transformation in the way marketers must think and act. At the same time, nothing has changed: marketers still work under immense time pressure, budgets are always constrained, and organizational structures often create a divide between product development, product marketing, branding, digital, and sales functions. In this playing field, marketers must find a way to create the right content and reach their audience in an effective way. This book is written for people who wish to transform the way marketing works. In line with its title, the book is not about theories or abstract models, but about pragmatic, effective ways that have been proven to make marketing more effective. In it, we provide easy-to-use tools and templates for the various steps we describe. This practical book is about making sure time and money are spent on the things that really matter, but most of all the book stresses the importance of getting to know your audience and engaging with them in a personal, relevant way.

The potential impact of person-to-person marketing is huge: Not only does it allow organizations to engage with new and existing customers in an effective way, nurturing brand preference and increased sales, it also effectively turns these customers into brand advocates. In this manner, the marketing team is in effect extended beyond the organization, amplifying the reach while being able to provide a personal, authentic message. The impact of this approach, measured in ROI and revenue, is substantial. As we will describe, the Cut the Bullsh*t marketing approach has resulted in campaigns that have generated up to $2,500 in sales opportunities for every dollar invested. Part of this book's story has been captured in a Stanford GSB case study that is used in executive and MBA education (Shiv & Hoyt, 2015). The success of the approach has been acknowledged by a broad range of peers and has resulted in various awards, including the 2015 ACE Award for B2B Account-based Marketing Excellence, the SABRE Award, and the Exhibitor Magazine's All-Star Award.

How to read this book

Short on time? Want the bottom line?
> Go for the sections indicated by the following markings.

Want to be an effective marketer who creates IMPACT and generates ROI?
> Read the whole book!

Want to create your own Cut the Bullsh*t marketing plan?
> Fill out the templates at the end of each chapter, bundle them, and go get results!

Our purpose with this book is to share our experiences and insights (from seemingly boring companies in the manufacturing industry) to help others with practical advice on marketing. We have included a wide range of real examples from the field to illustrate the various principles and to show what worked for us and what we learned. We strongly believe in these principles, as we have seen them work time and again in various business settings. With this book, we aim to inspire others to apply those principles, but mostly to go out and experiment! Cut the Bullsh*t Marketing is about doing, not about talking!

Structure of the book

The book is structured in five sections, reflecting the five key ingredients of Cut the Bullsh*t marketing: engaging on a personal level, understanding your customer, designing for engagement, going for it, and creating a Cut the Bullsh*t marketing organization. Thus, the first five sections are as follows:

1. *Make it personal!* – An introduction to Cut the Bullsh*t marketing – what it entails and where it can be applied (spoiler alert: in any business!).

2. *Understand your customer* – A deep understanding of who your customer is, how he or she works, and where you can add value. This is the single most important aspect of marketing.

3. *Design for engagement: Digitally & physically* – How to transform the customer's insights into an effective marketing experience. What approach and instruments can help to design for engagement?

4. *Go for it! Engage to the maximum! Examples from the field* – Stories of people-to-people marketing that worked for us. These anecdotes illustrate the principles of Cut the Bullsh*t marketing.

5. *Create a Cut the Bullsh*t marketing organization* – How to create a marketing organization for people-to-people marketing that is designed for ROI and revenue by putting the customer first.

The sixth section is about *the impact of Cut the Bullsh*t marketing*: return on investment and revenue. In this section, we also present six essential ingredients for measuring marketing impact.

Create your own Cut the Bullsh*t marketing plan

The book has been designed to help you create your own Cut the Bullsh*t marketing plan. Each chapter of the book ends with questions and templates that help you identify the essential ingredients of a tactical marketing plan. If you take these out and bundle them, you will have answered the following essential questions: Who are we targeting? What drives these people? What messages are they receptive to? What do we want to achieve? How will we measure the impact of the campaign?

Create your own Cut the Bullsh*t marketing plan

1. To start off, describe where you currently are with regard to marketing.

You

2. What is your marketing ambition? Where would you like to be in one year, or in five years? (P.S. Double-check yourself here: Did you cut out the bullsh*t?)

Create your own Cut the Bullsh*t marketing plan

3. How are you going to bridge the gap?

You

Notes

MAKE IT PERSONAL!

1

B2B and B2C are dead; people-to-people marketing is the way forward!

For years, people believed that marketing in a business-to-business (B2B) setting worked in a fundamentally different way than in a business-to-consumer (B2C) setting. For some aspects of marketing, that might be true. However, humans remain humans, and human decision-making is not that different in the two settings. When humans are involved, emotions will always be present, and this is as it should be. Also, in B2B settings, customers get a substantial amount of information from other customers, Internet groups, and discussion forums. For instance, 93% percent of B2B purchases start with an Internet search (Shiv & Hoyt, 2015). One could argue that because of the way people are getting used to service and engagement in the B2C space, the B2B space was forced to provide similar service and engagement as well, which makes the difference trivial: People-to-people marketing is founded on the awareness that real people drive decisions. Research shows that "71% of buyers who see a personal value in a B2B purchase will end up buying the product or service. Personal value, perhaps better read emotional value, had 2 times the impact on the buyer than business impact did, and overwhelmingly outweighed logic and reason in driving purchase decisions" (Newman, 2014).

Therefore, effectively managing social relationships with customers as people is critical and extremely effective.

The essence of people-to-people marketing was explored as early as 2001 at Washington University by Dr. Sandeep Krishnamurthy (2001). The merits of this approach have since been explored and documented, for instance by Carlos Hidalgo (2011) and Amy Sorrells (2013). Although there are plenty of models to explain how people-to-people marketing works, we like to focus on real examples – on experiments that proved to work for us – and share with you what we learned.

Two strategies, one vision: Know your customer

Marketing organizations typically adopt either a strategy aimed 1) toward serving a limited group of (key) accounts, or 2) toward serving a large group of customers who are typically unknown. The first strategy, which is also referred to as account-based marketing, is aimed at influencing the buying behavior of the customer accounts that are likely to order large quantities of your product or service. This is a limited group of accounts that can be served by a (key) account management team. This strategy is represented by the left-hand end in figure 1, indicating that there is a small group of customers with a large sales volume.

The second marketing strategy is focused on the so-called long tail (Anderson, 2006), as seen on the right-hand side of the graph. This strategy is aimed at serving the large group of customers who individually represent only a small sales volume but as a group represent a substantial market in terms of their total sales volume. The sales volume in the long tail may even exceed the sales volume of the large accounts. Amazon.com is an example of a brand that would be located on this side of the graph. In contrast to what people may initially expect, the long-tail strategy also requires knowledge about customers. We consider it even more important to understand these customers (individually), since there is hardly any personal contact through (key) account managers, and

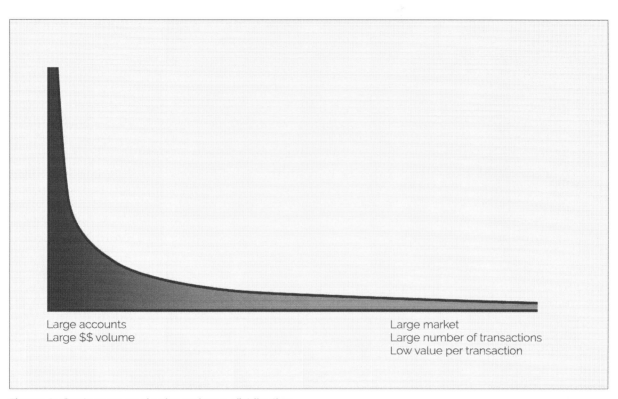

Large accounts
Large $$ volume

Large market
Large number of transactions
Low value per transaction

Figure 1: Customers and sales-volume distribution

the relationship is thus merely "digital." For instance, being able to recommend products based on an individual's previous behavior is an effective tool in this marketing strategy. The ability to engage with them on all social channels and community sites is also effective, as is being available with answers in case people ask questions. Those forms of engagement also provide deep insights into what a given customer needs. These insights can be used to create additional content that can in turn be used for the rest of the client base.

Both marketing strategies have their merits, and which one is most beneficial depends on your business and your market. However, in both models, understanding your target audience is essential and should be balanced with a healthy focus on revenue and impact. This forms the essence of our Cut the Bullsh*t marketing approach: **no-nonsense, pragmatic,** **customer centric,** and **focused on business impact.** Our Cut the Bullsh*t marketing approach has successfully been applied to both account-based marketing and long-tail marketing, while the way that the strategy is translated into tactics and marketing campaigns differs significantly.

People-to-people account-based marketing

Traditional account-based marketing pays significant attention to knowing and understanding the customer. Organizations that apply this model typically work with (key) account management teams that focus on a small group of customers who generate the most business. These account-management teams work in a people-to-people manner, providing their customers with tailored content that matches their specific business and context. This model can only scale in a linear way, as more customers can only be served by adding more resources.

Digitally, the same strategy is also possible (and more easily scalable): As soon as a visitor logs into your website or extranet, you can provide that visitor with content and functionality that matches his or her specific needs and context. The success of digital business portals fits this strategy and allows organizations to engage in digital people-to-people marketing.

Even when visitors to your website are not logged in, it is still possible to provide them with tailored content, for instance by translating their IP addresses to a business domain. We have done various tailored content marketing campaigns in which we measured effects in terms of engagement and sales opportunities. In the campaigns, we used IP address-identification technology to determine what company each visitor worked for. Based on business rules we created, the website then provided the visitor with content tailored to their specific needs. Using this technology, we could present a tailored web experience for visitors from hundreds of companies by customizing the home page experience, the messaging, and the content to their individual contexts. At the start, the approach challenged us to the maximum, as it resulted in immediate feedback on all of our assumptions about our visitors. Despite the steep learning curve, the program was successful, as it increased web downloads for application notes, datasheets, and software by 53%, and it increased sales-accepted opportunities from these target companies by 10% (Demandbase, 2017). This proved that digital account-based marketing strategies are possible and effective. The beauty of this is the potential to scale progressively without being restricted by resources. Here, technology assists in clever scaling. It also helps to cut out the bullsh*t for your customer. A customer only sees what he or she needs, in the language he or she speaks, and within the right context. He or she gets a personalized, contextualized, and localized red-carpet treatment. Who doesn't want that!

People-to-people long-tail marketing

One of the key questions when applying a people-to-people approach for a long-tail marketing strategy is how such a model can scale. Marketing departments (and technical support organizations), which already struggle with handling the key accounts and major customer segments, might be afraid that a people-to-people model would be impossible to achieve, given the enormous amount of time and effort that would cost. In our experience, a properly conducted mass-market people-to-people approach can actually reduce the amount of time and effort you have to spend. Key to this is that not just the marketing people will do the marketing; the whole company *and the community of existing customers* will join in the marketing efforts. Some of the campaigns we will describe in this book have achieved viral effects, or snowball effects, whereby people have spread a message (in a personal way) to their network, amplifying our reach tremendously.

Additionally, the Internet can be considered to be the largest call center in the world. If engagement is done correctly, people will help people. There is no larger pleasure than to be able to help other people. Peer recognition is an enormous driver. People helping people happens organically on all social sites, but it can also be stimulated by creating new community sites where people and experts help each other. The content experts in a company must be present online as collaborators, subject matter experts, moderators, and contributors. At Atmel, existing and newly created community sites took over large chunks of the technical support work that would normally hit a technical support organization. It helped them to scale proportionally and do more business with more customers at the same time.

There are no unglamorous products, only unimaginative solutions

While discussing viral campaigns and successful marketing examples, a frequently heard comment is: "Well, this would not work in my industry, as we have an unglamorous product." Our position on this is clear: There are no unglamorous products – only unimaginative solutions. With the right imaginative mindset, people-to-people marketing can be done for any product or service in any market. The way people are approached and treated, the ease of being able to do business with companies, the ability to reach out to peers can be key differentiators in marketing these products.

Sander Arts explains how he went about marketing semiconductors:

Sander
Arts

On the surface, a semiconductor isn't very sexy. It is a commodity product that has multiple applications, but it is not necessarily super appealing to people and mostly hidden from them. In my experience, semiconductors are always marketed in the same way. The market is told that the product has the best features, the lowest footprint (size), and the best power performance (low power). If that doesn't help close the deal, sales (and marketing!) people will emphasize the low price (the worst marketing!). It has always amazed me that the marketing for these amazingly technologically advanced products that take years and multiple billions of dollars

in R&D to develop and contain amazing intellectual property are sold like this. It always left me with an incredible feeling of failure to see a product being marketed like that. Didn't these products go into the world's most amazing machines and applications? Didn't they go to the moon? Didn't they give people the most incredible sensory experiences?

Why would the smartest people I've ever met in my life spend years developing an insanely great technology and then market it in the most amateurish way, as if it did not deserve the last step? Shouldn't we do justice to the care and effort people had put in? Why market it based on price? There was one more thing: This amazing technology was being created and improved at an insane pace, even as its price was being lowered continuously!

The strategy that I used as head of marketing was to bring the experience to the forefront more than the technology itself. The strategy involved tapping into people's passion for the simplicity and ease of use of our products. We would show how people used our products to create great experiences, how they brought the technology to life! This would catalyze engagement and content creation by our fan base. The result would be genuine stories and marketing the product beyond its technical specification and its price.

Therefore, we said at the beginning of our marketing journey, "Let's go and communicate the imaginative solutions that you could apply with this product and technology, and start to communicate those through stories." Let's celebrate the use of our technology, regardless of its application. We started putting spotlights on the hobby projects people created, and we also highlighted how people used our products to make the world a better place. With this approach, we managed to build a huge community of people, like a kind of fan base, in an industry that isn't used to having a fan base. The mindset within the marketing organization was we were a media company that sold semiconductors; this created brand preference, and leads.

I believe that you can apply the same thinking to all industries: Focus on the impact that your product could have in the marketplace or in people's lives.

> Remember, if we could do this for a commodity product like a semiconductor, then you can probably do it for any commodity in the world. There's no such thing as a boring product, but there are a lot of usual, unimaginative ways to market those products.

Tools for effective people-to-people marketing

In this chapter, we describe the importance of engaging in a people-to-people manner, regardless of whether your business is focusing on key accounts or on a long-tail strategy. In line with this approach, you need tools to capture customer insights in a structured and insightful manner, beyond the standard fields typical Customer Relationship Management tools apply. Instead, the tools discussed in this chapter aim to stimulate a more reflective way of capturing customer insights.

Instrument: Value proposition canvas

The value proposition canvas (Strategyzer AG, 2017; Osterwalder et al., 2014) is a visual canvas that helps in focusing on what drives your customer, what that customer needs, the products your organization offers, and how these are related.

To use the canvas, it is important to focus on the customer first; do not start by describing your own products and services. Therefore, we advise the following order of steps to apply this canvas.

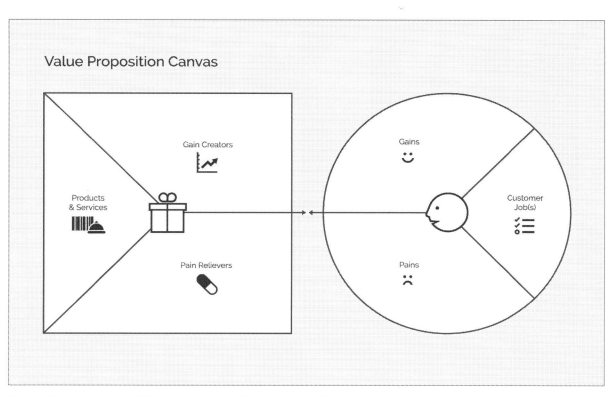

Figure 2: Value proposition canvas – by Strategyzer AG & strategyzer.com

Step 1: Describe the customer jobs.
In this box, you gather all the customer needs – that is, the problems they are trying to solve and the tasks they are trying to perform or complete.

Step 2: Describe the customer pains.
List all the negative emotions and the undesired costs, situations, and risks that the customer could experience before, during, and after getting the job done.

Step 3: Describe the customer gains.
Capture all the customer's benefits and desires. This may include personal, functional, and/or economical gains. For example, this box could include positive emotions, functional requirements, and/or specific cost savings.

Step 4: Describe the products and services.
At this point, it is good to describe all the products and services around which your value proposition is built. This includes, for example, the services that you offer or the functional, social, or emotional help the customer receives.

Step 5: Describe the pain relievers.
Now describe how your products and services address the challenges, needs, and pains of the customer and how you can eliminate negative emotions, undesired costs, and/or avoidable situations.

Step 6: Describe the gain creators.
Finally, capture how your products and services create gains and offer added value to your customer.

By completing these steps in this order, the value proposition canvas helps you think about your customer in a reflective way, thus providing a thoughtful foundation for your people-to-people marketing strategy.

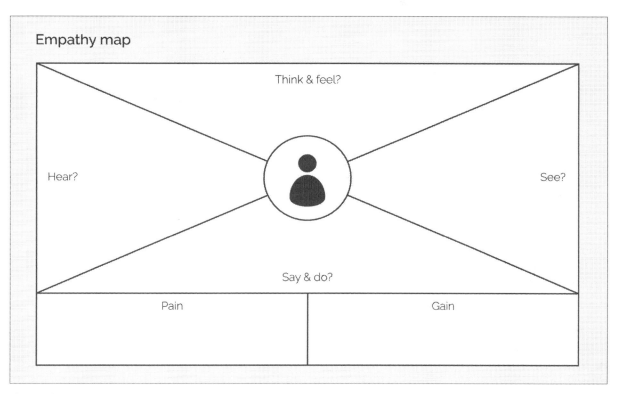

Figure 3: Empathy map

Instrument: Empathy map

An empathy map is another instrument that marketing teams can use to gain a deeper insight into their customers. Empathy maps help to shed light on which problems to solve and how. An empathy map can represent a group of users, such as a customer segment. The empathy map was originally created by Dave Gray et al. (2010) and published in their book *Gamestorming*.

Gamestorming also describes how to apply this instrument. As a brief summary of this recipe, here is the process we typically follow:

Step 1: Bring all that matters.
Gather all relevant stakeholders from marketing, sales, and customer experience and ask them to bring any customer descriptions, customer insight, or data they might have for the customer groups you will target.

Step 2: Map out the thoughts.
Print out or sketch the empathy map template on a large piece of paper or whiteboard. Hand each participant sticky notes and a marker. Each person should write down their thoughts on sticky notes. Ideally, everyone would add at least one sticky to every section. You might ask questions like the following:
- What would the user be thinking and feeling? What are some of the user's worries and aspirations?
- What would the user's friends, colleagues, and boss be likely to say if the user was using our product? What would the user hear in these scenarios?
- What would the user see while using our product in their environment?
- What might the user be saying and/ or doing while using our product? How

would that change in a public or private setting?
- What are some of the user's frustrations or fears when using our product?
- What gains might the user experience when using our product?

Have the team members speak about the sticky notes as they place them on the empathy map. Ask questions to elaborate deeper insights for the rest of the team.

Step 3: Make it personal.
In our experience, it helps to sketch out the characteristics this user may have on the center of the face in the template. Capturing such characteristics helps to establish the right tone of voice, to determine how to reach that customer, and to make the description a lot more about real human beings.

Step 4: Capture insights.
At the end of the session, ask the team members what insights they learned. More importantly, ask them what hypotheses they now have about the customers they would like to validate.

Instrument: C-P-S-P approach

A very powerful, yet simple way to structure propositions in line with customer expectations is to streamline it using four columns: Change leads to Problems that can be solved with Solutions, which consist of Products. This is the C-P-S-P approach.

Change: From a customer's point of view, what exactly is changing in his or her environment, market, or organization? Typically, this is about factors over which the customer has no direct influence and with which he or she must deal. Also, visionary ambitions can be listed here. Example: Introduce regulations for companies to become carbon dioxide neutral.

Problems: Change leads to a mismatch between the desired and current situation. This mismatch emerges either from the desired change (e.g. new company direction) or from external influences (e.g. market circumstances). Key here is the fact that the problems impact the daily decisions and actions of the customer. Example: Determine how to ensure that our logistic operations meet the new regulations by reducing emissions by 20%.

Solutions: Problems can be solved with solutions. A solution in this context consists of an integrated set of products, activities, and/or methods that result in an acceptable resolution of the problem/challenge. Example: Use low-emission vehicles and electric on- and off-loading.

Products: Products are the things or activities you are offering to your customer. Example: The new hybrid super truck has a low-emission engine and brake-energy regeneration.

By distinguishing between these four aspects, you become aware of the context of your customer, understand the problems he or she is facing, and clearly see what your organization offers. In our experience, the C-P-S-P approach is a good tool for stimulating outside-in thinking and for getting away from discussions that are too product focused.

Instrument: Effective story map

The previous tools help you to develop a good definition of the proposition and an initial understanding of the (potential) customer base. However, the result may be a complex set of ideas, requirements, propositions, and statements. In this complexity, which is very real, lies a pitfall if you want to avoid bullsh*t. You need a way to deal with this complexity, a way

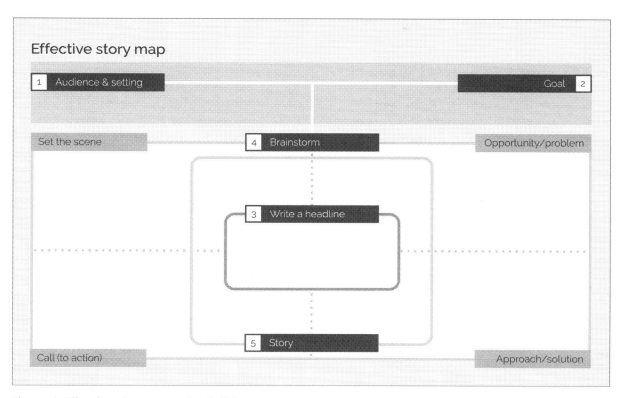

Figure 4: Effective story map – by GriDD

to embrace it without oversimplifying it or ending up with vague statements, unclear reasoning, and an ineffective story that does not resonate with people.

A powerful instrument for handling complexity is the effective story map. This tool, developed by GriDD, provides a framework for story architecture. Story architecture brings structure to a story and connects the goals and intended effects to the content at hand. By creating structure in the form of a mind map, you get a core story framework for your marketing that will provide the basis for all messaging and marketing activities.
The effective story map helps you quickly create a great story. Defining what you want to say and how you want to say it can be a challenge. With this model, you create a one-page overview of your storyline, while keeping focused on the goal, audience, and setting.

One benefit is that you can collaborate on the story with others, since this is a visual exercise. It provides a structure to deal with all requirements, ideas, content, and key statements you want to include, and it helps you transform these elements into a story that people will connect to.

Effective story map

Scan the QR code or go to www.cutthebullshit marketing.com/toolkit for a downloadable version of the effective story map.

Step 1: Audience and setting.
Describe the characteristics of the audience and the setting for your story. Write down what you know about the people and where and how they will receive this story.

Step 2: Set a goal/intended effect.
Describe what you want to accomplish by telling this story. What do you want the audience to remember, do, or feel?

Step 3: Write a headline.
Write down the desired end result. Write a headline that indicates the content of the story. This is what your story is all about. Writing it down like a newspaper headline ensures its clarity.

Step 4: Brainstorm.
Brainstorm story elements by making a mind map around the headline. Write your story in statements. Include statements about four elements: 1) Setting the scene (Why do you want to tell this story? What is the motivation?), 2) Opportunity/problem (What is the opportunity you see? What problem is this story is about?), 3) Approach/solution (What approach will you take? What is the solution to the problem?), and 4) Call to action (What do you want people to do?).

Step 5: Story.
Create a story by prioritizing statements. Highlight the core statements and/or place them closest to the headline. The further away a statement is from the headline, the less important it is to the story.

Tips:
- Write down a first and a last sentence, so you will always have a strong start and finish.
- When prioritizing statements, keep in mind the goal, audience, and setting.
- If needed, use an empty template to order and rewrite statements in step 5.
- Draw this model on a whiteboard and use sticky notes. This allows you to move statements around easily and thus create a comprehensive story.
- Create a story together by using this model during a group session.

Conclusion

Thinking in terms of B2C and B2B is dead. In business settings, marketing should be focused on the people involved and on their emotions. Whether you apply an account-based marketing, distribution marketing, or long-tail marketing model, it is essential to understand the people you are targeting and to communicate with them in a personal manner (at scale). Only then does marketing resonate, generating impact and revenue. Making it personal is the foundation of Cut the Bullsh*t marketing approach, which promotes no-nonsense, customer-centric, and business-impact-focused marketing. Key instruments include the value proposition canvas, which helps you focus on the people you are targeting, their pains, and the gains they are after. In the next chapter, we will further elaborate on getting to understand your customer.

Create your own Cut the Bullsh*t marketing plan

4. Who is your target audience?

5. What is the most important group you are aiming for?

You

Create your own Cut the Bullsh*t marketing plan

6. For a typical member of this group, fill out an empathy map:

You

Empathy map

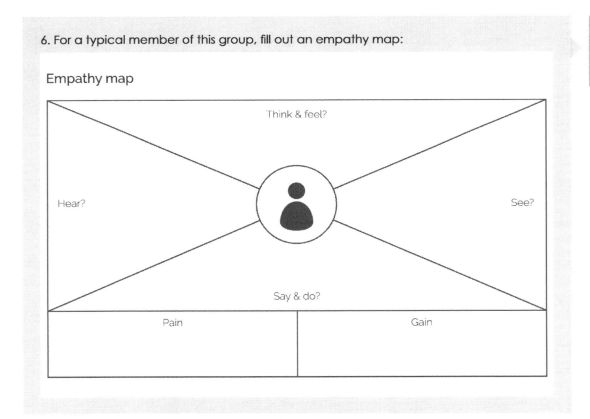

Think & feel?

Hear?

See?

Say & do?

Pain

Gain

Create your own Cut the Bullsh*t marketing plan

7. What is your proposition?
What do you bring your customers in relation to their pains and gains?

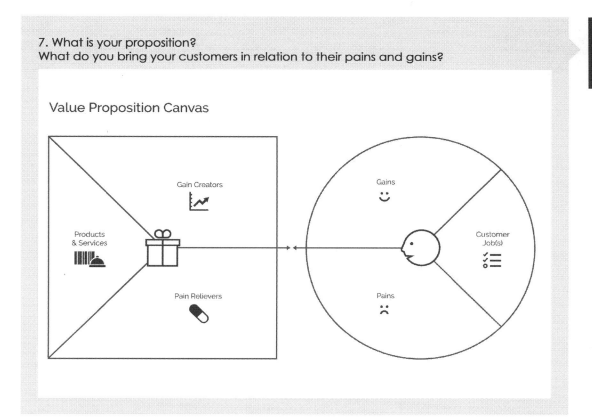

Value Proposition Canvas

Gain Creators

Products & Services

Pain Relievers

Gains

Customer Job(s)

Pains

You

Create your own Cut the Bullsh*t marketing plan

Notes

You

UNDERSTAND YOUR CUSTOMER

2

Understanding your customer is the single most important aspect of successful marketing. Any successful people-to-people marketing effort starts with knowing who your customer is, what their work is, what drives them, how they would like to work (even if that is not yet a reality), and how your product could fit into their work and life. This section is about getting to know your customers and their activities. We describe how to use rich persona descriptions and customer activity cycles to capture insights and to guide marketing design decisions.

Get to know the person to target

Before anything else in marketing, you need to know who you are targeting. This seems obvious, but organizations have traditionally focused on key accounts and large customer segments, in which the number of people to know was quite limited. The shift to a people-to-people approach also has huge consequences for how you go about gaining insights into your customers. Traditionally, marketers would call or visit selected accounts to gain a rich image of their contacts, who were typically buyers at a medium to large organization. This personal contact is the essence of successful marketing. However, in people-to-people marketing, your target audience is much broader and typically involves not just the person who buys your product but also the people who use your product. These different groups require different approaches and different marketing content.

The increased scale of your audience makes it difficult or impossible to nurture personal contact in the way account management used to work. Therefore, new approaches are needed, leveraging the possibilities of digital tools and building on personal (social) networks. Keys to our approach include capturing insights about the people we are targeting in the persona descriptions and investigating how they work and how they prefer to do business. These insights demand customer research – that is, interviews and surveys with actual customers. We have also tried gaining these insights via the sales and customer service departments. However, getting such information "by proxy" did not work for us, as it creates an incomplete, biased image of the customer.

When investigating whom to target, the first question to ask is which customers are relevant to your business and how important each type of customer is to your business. When this is clear, step away from abstract descriptions of this customer type and focus on actual people. Who are they? What drives them? One needs to understand that these people have multiple facets. For example, one target customer might be an engineer who is also a father of two children and a model-railway enthusiast. If you understand this and engage target customers based on their multiple facets, your message will be much likelier to resonate with them, and, ultimately, you will sell more of your products.

Sander Arts explains how this notion helped him realize he had to engage with the so-called maker community:

Sander
Arts

What we learned is that the persona of a customer does not fit a single description. When we talk about people-to-people marketing, we're trying to be as personal as can be. As a result, we have to try and understand the many facets of each individual.

Let me give you an example. At Atmel, we found that a large pro-portion of users of our technology also participated in the so-called maker community. The maker community is a very large group of people from all over the world who share a passion for making things. These people have a drive to make the world a better place, have fun, and share experiences. The Maker Faires that happen across the globe are the world's largest show-and-tell events and attract hundreds of thousands of visitors. It is a true community of people who all have a passion for sharing and making. Within that community, there is a large group of technology users. One of the open source communities within the larger group of makers works and creates projects based on Arduino development boards. Those boards (essentially small computers) are built around an Atmel microcontroller. People would make anything and every-thing and share the code so that colleague makers could take it and build on it, making something else. It was a true celebration of our technology, and we decided to build a large company presence at those Maker Faires globally.

To give you an example, there was a particular Maker Faire in San Mateo, CA, where more than 130,000 people visited over a single weekend. At this Maker Faire, a gentleman came to me and spoke about the Atmel microcontroller on the Arduino board and how he uses it on weekends to build projects with his child. Basically, he and his child were creating an Arduino-powered Halloween costume.

Figure 5: Impressions of Maker Faires [1]

[1] Picture on the left by Chester: https://www.flickr.com/photos/chesterbr/15240656974
Picture on the right by Kevin Jarrett: https://www.flickr.com/photos/kjarrett/15302938331

Later in the conversation, it turned out that this gentleman was also one of the lead engineers at a very large equipment-manufacturing company. When he had to decide which micro-controller to put into a high-selling product, he decided to include that particular microcontroller into his design, since he had had exposure to our microcontrollers through his hobby projects. For us, it was important to realize that fathers or mothers who visit a Maker Faire take some of that experience with them to work. We figured that out early on and built a company presence at the Faire. We managed to engage on a whole dif-ferent level with our customers, fo-cused on their passion for making and building awesome projects. We started writing about these projects. We started to share people's passion. We started tapping into a whole new world – an entirely new customer base – in an entirely new way. Nobody had ever marketed semiconductors this way. It was wildly successful, as we were able to create one of the largest fan bases in the world around a semiconductor brand. We started to nurture these people and market to them, and in so doing enlarged the customer base in the long tail for the company.

Therefore, I encourage people to create persona descriptions that are as rich as possible so that they can understand that a main engineer at an A-level manufacturing firm working on IoT (Internet of Things) solutions could also, on the weekend, be a maker doing hobby projects or a consumer of lighthearted, engineering-focused content on a blog or other social media outlet.

Obviously, you cannot create 30,000 individual persona descriptions, so you will have to settle for just a few. However, make sure these persona descriptions capture the broad facets of the people you are targeting so that you are able to engage with them on multiple levels using dedicated pieces of content, which you will have to create.

Application to business: Persona descriptions

A persona is a fictional character that represents a potential user, and it is created from the results of customer research that is based on a user-centered design process. A persona description includes a photo, a story, and a discussion of the personality and the relevance to the subject of the design. In this way, persona descriptions do the following:

- Help frame design questions according to more specific user considerations
- Allow a team to live and breathe the user's world
- Provide focus and create a frame of reference
- Provide input during discussions from the customers' perspective
- Evaluate ideas and designs along the way
- Help decide on inevitable design trade-offs
- Enable better tactical-level design decisions
- Provide a powerful method to engage with complex audiences

Persona Canvas

1 Personal profile

Age, family, profession, job role, residence...

2 Media preference

Attitude, interest, media use...

3 Relation to product/business

Publicity, reputation, how to make his/her life easier?

4 Knowledge & proficiency

Education, speciality

5 Specific goals, needs, attitude

Drives, interest, what is making him/her happy?
What is his/her vision in life?

6 Picture

What does he/she looks like?
Choose a picture and put it here

7 Quote

What is a typical statement?

8 Offline

Where do we meet offline?

Figure 6: Persona canvas – by GriDD

Persona canvas

 Scan the QR code or go to www.cutthebullshit marketing.com/toolkit for a downloadable version of the persona canvas.

We typically apply the following process to get to a set of persona descriptions:

Step 1: Perform interviews/customer research
- Ideally, persona descriptions should be based on interviews and direct observation of customers.
- Other sources, which should be handled with care, are customer surrogates (domain experts/trainers), informants and interpreters (marketing, sales, or documentation experts), and indirect sources (manuals, artifacts, or questionnaires).

Step 2: Create draft descriptions
- Use a template to kick-start your persona descriptions. The template in Figure 4 guides you through the first descriptions of the persona. Create separate persona descriptions for the different groups you encountered in step 1.

Step 3: Discuss and interact to refine
- Discuss the first draft. Prioritize the personas (focal/secondary, etc.).
- Make a final selection of key personas (a number between five and eight is manageable). These personas will have differences in terms of key characteristics. Visualize these diffe-rences to explain the playing field these personas cover. An example of how key characteristics can be mapped is shown in Figure 7.
- Elaborate on the persona's charac-teristics and refine.

Step 4: Visualize and present to relevant stakeholders
- Visualize the persona's profile. Make it personal by including a photo or an illustration of the persona and make sure the description is as clear as possible. As an example, see Figure 8.

- Present final persona descriptions to whomever will be working with the personas and fill those people in the details.

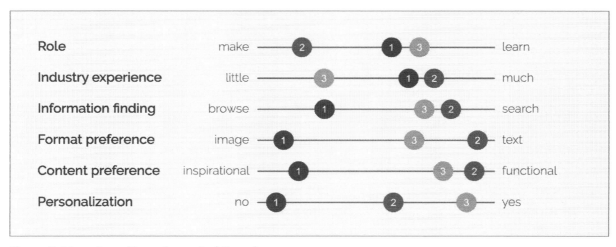

Figure 7: Mapping of key characteristics of personas

Heike

"I have a passion for home automation and love to talk with my customers on all exciting possibilities."

Heike is 30 years old, single and lives in her apartment in a large city. She is a third party sales agent, responsible for connected home automation systems. Heike reads a lot about the internet of things (IoT) and experiments with smart home applications in her own apartment.

Knowledge and job activities
- Heike has been working as a sales agent for 2 years now. After graduation she started working in sales support, but started working as sales agent pretty soon after.
- Heike loves to work with people and likes to work with customers on the scope of the projects and discuss product suggestions.
- She sometimes works with technology designers and engineers for drawings and specifications.

Media / communication preferences
- She likes to put through requests by phone to sales support, since that saves her a lot of time. Usually she briefs products and desired configurations.
- In her spare time she spends a lot of time on the internet to read about cool new IoT projects.

Specific goals and attitudes
- Heike wants to offer her customers competitive pricing. Whenever the quotes people can't go below certain levels they turn to zone quote leads that decide on pricing.
- Since she works closely with her customers she always wants to return an offer as soon as possible to keep her customer happy.

Tooling preferences and needs
- After Heike sends the quote to her customer some additional negotiations take place and the quote needs to be revised. If she would be using a tool it should support revisions and should generate revision references.

Figure 8: Persona example

Understand your customer's bigger picture

For the person you are targeting, your product is part of a bigger picture: Your product is a part of their activities, but there are bigger processes involved. To successfully engage with your target audience, you have to understand the bigger picture. The instrument we apply for this is describing a customer activity cycle. This instrument and approach has been described in detail by Sandra Vandermerwe (2000) in *MIT Sloan Management Review*.

Mark
Geljon

We adopted the customer activity cycle, as described by Sandra Vandermerwe, as a way to really understand the daily activities of our customers and to identify

lock-ons and lock-outs – that is, points in the customer's process when our service can help them become an engaged customer or when they will move away because they are frustrated. This approach really helped us think from outside-in in a world where thinking from inside-out was the norm.

To create a customer activity cycle, we did a session with a number of people from within the company who are close to the customers: account managers, sales managers, and – very importantly – some real customers. Note that this group need not be large: In fact, even just 10 participants will give you vital insights, while still allowing for good discussions and collaborative brainstorming.

47

We asked the customers to demonstrate how they do their work and, almost as a task analysis, paid attention to the steps they took: How did they order? What did they do to select a vendor? What did they do when they wanted to know more about a product? What did they do once a project started? Basically, we ran them through the normal phases of their work. With this input, we drafted a customer activity cycle of their continuous process.

The result helped us to create a shared view on the activities of the customers and of the roles involved. For instance, it helped us to understand how electronic design projects work. After creating this first version of a customer activity cycle, we validated it with a large group of real customers (in our case, with thousands of engineers)

to validate the steps, get their input, and make it more specific for different roles. Role specificity is needed to gain insight into the consequences of your marketing touchpoints. It also enables you to offer information tailored to the job roles of the different people involved.

With this approach, we were able to improve our touchpoints and match them more specifically to our customers' needs.

Application to business: Customer activity cycle

The objective of a customer activity cycle is to provide insight into the full process of a customer. In the context of engineering, this could be from the earliest envisioning of a new product, all the way to delivery and after-care. A customer activity cycle creates a shared view for everything involved in the stages of the process, the activities in these stages, and possible lock-ons. Creating a customer activity cycle in a visual way makes it:

- Easier to digest
- Easier to drill down
- Easier to have a shared view/common understanding

In order to create a customer activity cycle, we typically use the following steps:

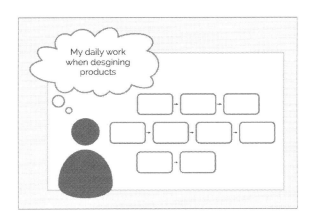

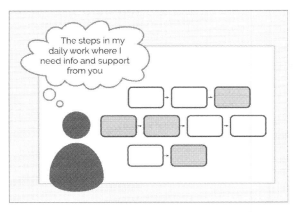

Step 1: Perform a task analysis

The first step is to conduct a task analysis with real customers (selected based on the persona descriptions) to understand their current ways of working and the information needs they have.

Visualize the customer activity cycle, for instance, using the template by GriDD, presented in Figure 9.

Step 2: Identify touchpoints

Identify the touchpoints within the flow of activities. These touchpoints represent moments when your product or information regarding your product is needed.

Describe the touchpoints in the activity cycle.

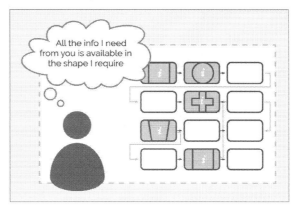

Step 3: Define needs

Define what products, tools, and information the customer needs at the various touchpoints to work most effectively. Pay extra attention to the form in which this needs to be provided for it to be most effective.

Add this information to the activity cycle.

Use the insights gathered in the activity cycle to provide your customer with the products, tools, and information in the right shape at the right moment.

To make the steps more practical, let us look at an example. In this case, we are working for a manufacturer of safety systems. In order to understand a key customer type (civil engineers), we construct a customer activity cycle about a particular civil engineer who constructs bridges. His specialty is bridges that include advanced technologies. He mainly works in rural areas for relatively small roads. Although no two projects are the same and the order of the steps can vary, overall his daily work includes the following:

- Looking for potentially useful technologies
- Understanding the market (which suppliers of bridge elements are interesting)
- Knowing which events to attend to be inspired by new technologies and to meet new and existing potential partners
- Being informed about legislation regarding safety and the environment
- Creating a concept design for a new bridge
- Looking for technologies to include in concept designs
- Calculating the specifics of bridge designs
- Managing relationships with stakeholders of current projects (environment, local municipality, etc.)
- Briefing management about the business case of a project
- Briefing the construction team with the specifics of a bridge
- Assisting maintenance teams with specific challenges in existing bridges
- Discussing with partners the specific solutions for design problems

By executing a detailed task analysis, this list can easily grow to 80+ tasks, depending on the individual's role. By clustering these into main areas, the sections of the customer activity cycle can be defined. In this case, one could state that "keep up to date," "conceptualize," "select partners and technologies," "getting buy-in," and "after-care" are relevant areas. These are the main phases of the cycle in which all the relevant activities are inserted.

At this point, it is time to scope. What activities in the analysis are relevant to us as a supplier? In the example above, "relationship management" might be an activity in which we are not involved. We must define the touchpoints in these scoped activities. Where does the civil engineer go to perform the activity? Here, we include both physical and digital places. What value can we bring to these activities so that our customer is supported in doing his job? As a manufacturer of safety systems, we should not only support him with the actual delivery of our safety systems, but we should also provide information that helps him convince the management of the use of certain technologies and provide reference information for maintenance.

Having defined how we can support our customer, we now need to design and create the tools and resources to make this work. For example, we could create an app for referencing our safety systems, we could create an extranet for maintenance, and we could decide to be present in relevant magazines with our innovations. In this way, we are truly supporting our customer, creating immediate value – and with that, brand preference and new opportunities as well.

Customer activity cycle canvas

Scan the QR code or go to www.cutthebullshit marketing.com/toolkit for a downloadable version of the canvas.

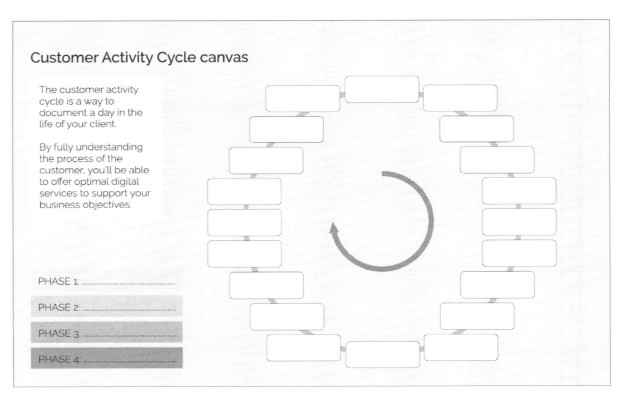

Customer Activity Cycle canvas

The customer activity cycle is a way to document a day in the life of your client.

By fully understanding the process of the customer, you'll be able to offer optimal digital services to support your business objectives.

PHASE 1: ....
PHASE 2: ....
PHASE 3: ....
PHASE 4: ....

Figure 9: Customer activity cycle canvas – by GriDD

Understand how your customer works

Whereas a customer activity cycle provides an overview of the phases in your customer's work and the activities involved, it does not (and should not try to) provide rich detail about the work activities of the people involved. Nevertheless, having this detailed understanding is essential to understanding how your products or information fits into the customer's daily activities, especially in a people-to-people marketing setting.

Unfortunately, we have been in various organizations for which the marketing departments created their customer understanding based on what they heard from the sales departments or the customer support desks. This way of gathering information by proxy reveals only a part of the image, and sometimes it provides a distorted image.

We have also made this mistake. Customer research takes time and money, and it opens you up to possible negative feedback as well. Now, armed with these experiences, we realize that the only way really to understand your customers is to approach them directly, hold interviews, perform a survey, or observe them as they work.

A nice example of the latter ethnographic approach is the campaign we ran in which we asked engineers to share pictures of their workbenches; this gave us a better understanding of the physical environments they were working in.

Jeroen Grit explains how this approach helped to design a matching customer experience:

Jeroen
Grit

As part of one of our projects, we wanted to provide engineers with easy access to documentation while working on prototypes. To determine what information they needed, and to understand the physical context properly, we conducted a campaign in which we invited engineers to share photographs of their workbench.

From the input we received, we gained valuable insights. We noticed that the laptop or the computer was not an integral part of the workbench. Instead, many engineers had two environments: a place for experimenting and a separate environment for doing

digital work on very large screens. The latter was useful input for the design team working on the website; it helped us make sure our interface would work well on screens with a broad range of resolutions. However, in addition to soldering or working on a prototype, the engineers also worked on paper; they would print out a lot of information from various websites. This supported our assumption that we could assist them with an iPad app that allowed them to collect documentation from our own website, from other websites, and from their personal document folders. We designed an app that would allow them to collect the relevant documents and specification sheets, put them on virtual piles, and have that information available at the click of a button or a tap on the screen while experimenting.

Figure 10: Example of a typical workbench (Picture by Phillip Burgess, https://www.flickr.com/photos/paintyourdragon/8133907832/)

Application to business: Stimulating user-generated content

Many professionals like to share pictures (or even videos) of their working environment. Even if the work happens completely in a digital environment, it is valuable to know in what setting your customer is working: Is he or she working in a busy office space, on the road frequently, or often working from a home office? Pictures can tell you a lot about the context of your customer and help you to target your marketing in a way that fits their routines.

Get down from your ivory tower

Understanding people's needs can only be done with their help. In what steps of your customers' process do they need support? Where is the overlap between their user needs and your business

57

needs? What does that mean for your products and services? Do they fit these needs or should you tailor your offerings? Understanding this fully can only be done together with your customers. Therefore, marketers must get out of their offices, go to customers, talk with them, learn about their needs, get them involved to test campaigns, and sit with them to click through wireframes or interact with a beta version of the product.

Mark Geljon explains how the beta approach helped to gather input from customers:

Mark
Geljon

We applied the beta approach as an answer to another approach that we were not satisfied with. That first approach focused on outlining all kinds of user scenarios. There we were, with a list of 75 user scenarios, describing what kind of functions the new website needed to fulfill, and that was before the concept of user stories even existed. This included statements like "I want to look at a data sheet to check the specifications" and "I want to order a sample so I can validate my assumptions." We first tried to get these user scenarios prioritized by the engineering community. The feedback we received included statements such as "I don't need a lot of marketing bullsh*t," "I find it very important to download a data sheet and less important to cross-reference information," and "I find it extremely important to have price information." We tried to build a website based on that information. The resulting website was very complex, because all these routes and journeys were interlinked, and we had all kinds of corporate limits on what the functionality of the website should look like and how it should work.

A tremendous amount of energy was put into it, and the results were good, but not as groundbreaking as we expected. When our part of the organization split off and became a separate organization, we had the opportunity for a greenfield approach. We could build a completely new semiconductor environment, but this time we would follow a different approach.

Convinced of the need to involve the engineering community from the first moment, we applied a beta approach. Using a beta approach in a corporate setting is not trivial, because you have two main audiences, one being the outside world, and the other being the inside world, the internal organization. We put a lot of effort into consolidating the feedback from these two audiences – both internal stakeholders and external stakeholders such as local marketing leaders, distributors, and engineers. After consolidating the information, we learned that the only way to solve the puzzle was to involve our target audience.

The beta approach had a couple of phases. In the first phase, the design phase, we involved internal and external focus groups to discuss specific complex functionality. For example, we did this when designing the selection guide, which is also known as the parametric search. In the semiconductor environment, this is a very complex function that allows you to select components based on their specifications. By creating wireframes and clickable prototypes, we validated our assumptions with our customers and got input on what worked and what did not. At the start of the design phase, we had assumptions about how to present parametric search results. It turned out that our customers wanted sliders. Because of this, we had to redo our design. From a functionality point of view, the redesign was very easy to achieve, but from a content point of view, it created all kinds of issues because of the data structures involved. We had to go back to the source – that is, to the engineers in our own organization – to make sure that we unified the parameters and had comparable products so the process could work properly. We could only do this because the feedback was out in the open, and because we under-

stood that being able to search for products this way was very important for our customers. The feedback helped us to understand what should get priority from our customers' perspective, and that helped us to focus on the right things.

In the second phase, the building phase, we used an incremental development approach. We launched a new beta website and let that run in parallel alongside the normal corporate website. We added buttons on the corporate website inviting visitors to visit the new website, even at the time when only a few parts of the new website were available. For instance, we would guide visitors to the new design of the product pages that included more consolidated, relevant information and that were less siloed around various content sources. In that way, we were already adding value to our customers, even in an environment that was not yet finalized.

On the beta website, we ran a feedback form engine so you could provide qualitative responses from the page you were on. We worked a lot with open feedback and sometimes cringed away from the feedback that was entered by the users. Nevertheless, the team would take it up and discuss what we wanted to do with it, checking if it was feasible and responding on the feedback platform so that people understood we received their feedback and acted upon it. We couldn't ignore feedback; it was out in the open for all to see.

Meanwhile, we collected these user requirements in a mind map, which we used to create separate branches for separate topics: performance, user experience, data quality, and so on. Each topic contained all the requirements that we distilled from the internal organization and from customer feedback. If we decided to postpone a certain functionality, we could see in the mind map who we needed to involve or who we needed to update about that decision and what the impact of that decision would be from a stakeholder's perspective.

Combining the beta approach with a mind map of requirements in this way gave us an option to drill down to the relevant details when needed, while keeping a high-level overview. Being able to track which stakeholder had what concerns helped us in stakeholder management.

Now, you may think that a process like this costs a lot of money and time. In our experience, it does indeed takes a few months. However, when designing the key point of interaction for your customers, it is often worth the investment: If you fail to provide your customers with the information they need and in the format they need, they are likely just to switch to a competitor. Understanding your customers' needs is therefore crucial.

Requirement management

 Scan the QR code or go to www.cutthebullshit marketing.com/toolkit for a downloadable version of the poster about require-ment management via mind maps: Grit, 2011.

Create a holistic picture

As illustrated in the previous section, it is essential to develop a holistic view of the user feedback provided. This holistic view is needed to see the impact of decisions from the perspective of various stakeholders. Grouped by topic, this one overview allows us to drill down to specific requirements, know from whom requirements originate, and see how the requirement impacts stakeholders. Collecting feedback in a mind map has proven to work well for us. The linked, hierarchical structure allows for communication about requirements on different levels of detail, while still providing the opportunity to delve into detail when needed.

Jeroen Grit explains how he created a holistic picture while managing complexity:

Jeroen
Grit

To gather user feedback, we typically conduct surveys with qualitative questions that ask people what they like, what they don't like, and what could be improved. From these surveys, we get a lot of different types of feedback: We get people talking about various things on our website, about the brand in general, and about our products. We sometimes received thousands of responses. I remember one survey for which we had around 8,000 respondents, and all had shared multiple open answers. We created a process in which five of us manually categorized these answers into about 20 categories.

Then, in a second stage, we picked a category – for instance, regarding the search functionality – and clustered the feedback into subcategories such as feedback regarding what they liked about the current search and what could be improved. This served as valuable input for a separate project to optimize the search function on the website.

The same approach worked well to capture feedback during an extensive set of interviews. We categorized the comments, created subcategories, and made sure each item was understandable and provided enough context. We also applied tags to facilitate filtering by topic, type of content, type of touchpoint, or source of feedback.

Since the mind map could be exported as a spreadsheet, we could use this document in improvement projects. A filter search would then allow us quickly to get an overview of all relevant feedback and even pinpoint its source.

Obviously, when you categorize thousands of different items, sometimes things do not get labeled correctly. Part of the strength of the method is in the numbers, so if you do not correctly categorize a few items, that is not a big deal, and correcting the labeling is very easy. Therefore, going through the feedback in the first round can be a fairly crude process. Then, if you revisit the mind map when starting a project, you can always select some of the related topics to see if there are additional items in there as well.

Conclusion

Understanding your customer is the single most important aspect of successful marketing. This understanding can only be gained in direct interaction with customers: interviews, surveys, focus groups, or direct observations. The key points to focus on include the following: What does the work process or decision process of the customer look like? In what steps of their process do they need support? Where do they get their information? Who do they involve or consult? What is the overlap between your customers' needs and your business offering? What does that mean for your products and services? Do your products fit these needs or should you tailor your offerings?

Create your own Cut the Bullsh*t marketing plan

8. How deep is your current understanding of the people you are targeting?

You

9. What are the key aspects of your customers that need a deeper understanding?

Create your own Cut the Bullsh*t marketing plan

10. What instruments/methods fit you and your customer, allowing you to capture a holistic image of the people you are targeting?

Notes

You

DESIGN FOR ENGAGEMENT: DIGITALLY & PHYSICALLY

3

Now that you are armed with insights about the people you are targeting, it is time to apply your marketing magic to design how you are going to engage these people. This is a magical step, but it is not magic! This is the point when the creation takes place – when you combine your insights with your experience and creativity to come up with something that draws attention, is worth sharing, and triggers people to act. Although there is no silver bullet for this part of the process, there are three guiding principles of effective marketing campaigns:

1. **Design for an optimized customer experience** – Building on customer insights, take the viewpoints of the people you are targeting, and include both the necessary interactions and the important channels in your campaign. However, focus on those interactions and channels that really create impact and revenue; leave out the bullsh*t!

2. **Design for an integrated approach** – Your customers operate in a world that is a blend of digital and physical aspects. Therefore, you should combine the digital and the physical in your campaigns and marketing activities, with consistent interactions that strengthen the message.

3. **Design for continuous change** – Both the world you are operating in and the people you are targeting are changing constantly, so your engagement should be agile! Gaining customer understanding is not a one-time activity; it must be a part of a continuous improvement cycle.

In the following sections, we elaborate on these three principles and describe how we applied them and what we learned.

Optimize the customer experience

As individual employees gain decision-making power in an organization, it becomes more important to make sure that they are properly served; you must offer them the information they need, in the format they need, and at the moment they need it. Armed with the insights captured from the persona descriptions and the customer activity cycle, we have a basis to understand what an optimized customer experience would mean for the daily work of the people we are targeting. With this, we can provide the right information at the right touchpoints by focusing on the interactions and touchpoints that really create an impact while leaving out the bullsh*t! If you manage to optimize the customer experience, your customers will find it easy to do business with you, which in turn will increase your revenue.

Mark Geljon explains how persona descriptions fueled the right discussions:

Mark
Geljon

In redesigns, we always work with personas. It is not just about having personas; it is about creating a design framework in which personas help to include the customer perspective, so as to guide and validate designs. Armed with this rich contextual information, we can design optimized digital experiences for specific types of users. We can basically steer the whole concept toward an integral and optimized digital engine – a digital experience.

How do we do that? Using persona descriptions during the design process, we can literally say, "Well okay, but how would Russell feel about this?" Russell, like the other personas, is – virtually – present during the design sessions; it is almost as if he is taking part in the discussions. In this way, we can focus on what really makes a difference in the customer experience. This proved very powerful, for instance, when we were designing a selection guide (also known as a parametric search). It turned out that, for our distributor persona, it was very important to learn about related products, as he needed that information to advise his clients. Without his perspective, we might have missed that aspect altogether.

Taking the integral design approach by constantly mapping out designs to the personas' needs opens up business-tactic discussions.

Instead of discussions about the color of the menu bar, the discussions were about why a main persona was not served with a specific type of content. Only by applying the persona approach could we make sure that the various customer perspectives were taken into account. This resulted in designs that provided the right information, in the right format, and at the right moment for the key users of the website. In turn, that improved conversion.

Instrument: UX concept approach

An important step in designing for engagement is to combine customer insights and design a user experience (UX) concept. A UX concept facilitates in the creation of a consistent experience throughout each customer's journey across various touchpoints. It provides direction – for instance, for a campaign implementation team or a website implementation team. Finally, it helps you formulate a goal to work toward.

Step 1: Capture and combine require-ments and UX research insights.
As described in the previous chapter, the first step is to understand your customer. The key insights from this research, inclu-ding the persona descriptions and key user requirements, should be combined with business requirements and content & design requirements (such as those for branding).

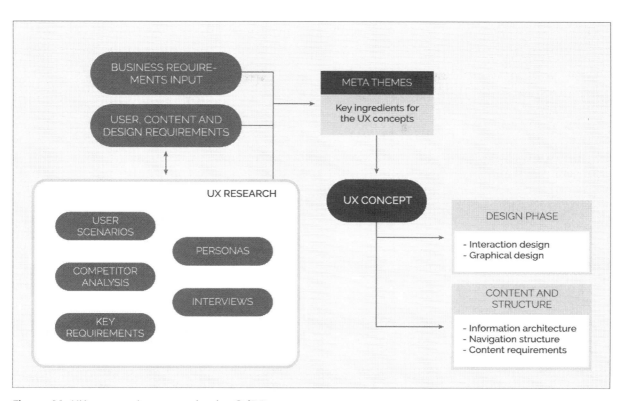

Figure 11: UX concept approach – by GriDD

Step 2: Define meta themes
From there, meta themes can be created to reflect all the relevant findings from the research and to steer the design, content, and structure. A good approach when constructing meta themes is to collect all key insights and to cluster them in three to seven stacks that have a common theme (such as "put the customer in the middle," or "support the work process"). These labels will be the meta themes. Write down these themes and create storylines for each theme and across the themes.

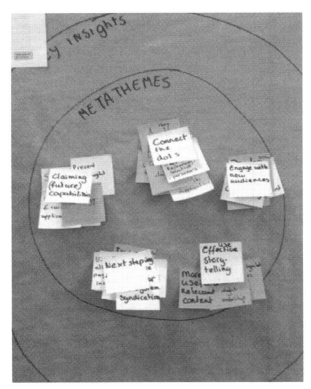

Figure 12: Example of constructing meta themes

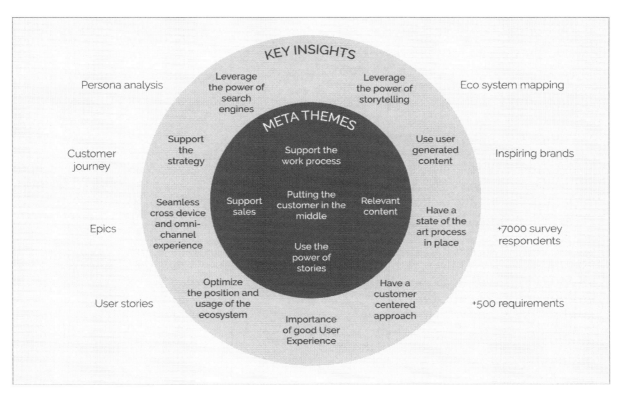

Figure 13: Example of bringing it all together

Integrate the approach

An important principle when designing people-to-people marketing is to take an approach that reaches people both digitally and physically – at all important points along their journey. The online and offline marketing instruments you design should amplify each other while providing a consistent message. We refer to this as "Pirates of the Caribbean marketing": marketing that reaches you wherever you are, with a recognizable and consistent "face." When Disney launched the movie Pirates of the Caribbean, the market was blasted with its marketing materials, including flyers, posters, digital campaigns, YouTube trailers, and merchandise. Wherever you were and whoever you were, you were exposed to the marketing material to make sure that you went to see the movie.

Sander
Arts

A nice example of how we went about reaching people both digitally and physically was by launching a fully equipped mobile trailer and taking it to key people, customers, and events so that we could hit our existing and potential customers. Our aim was to target the US market, which is large and in which the customers are spread around. We had a traditional way of conducting technical training. Every year, the same number of people would be trained on the latest products in the same cities. I then went and asked for a heat map based on our website. I wanted to know where the people who visited the website were physically located. It turned out that there was a large discrepancy between where we trained and where our (potential) customers were located.

Equipping an "Apple Store on wheels" made sense to me. We went and visited all those people. We cut through all the bullsh*t and simply showed up at their doors! The mobile trailer helped us in reaching these customers, even in remote locations. Able to house 35 attendees at a time in a classroom setup, the vehicle was equipped with enough comforts (such as Internet connectivity) to host the extensive training sessions that would take place inside. In fact, the trailer was outfitted in a way that allowed it to seamlessly transition from a mobile conference room into a content-creation platform, a technical-support center, a product-demo station, or a "hackathon" site – and everything in between. It generated audiences ranging from 35 to 200 students, engineers, teachers, or inventors. Wrapped in can't-miss Atmel-blue graphics, the massive tractor-trailer also doubled as a moving billboard that would raise brand awareness even between its event stops. In its first year, the truck covered more than 75,000 miles on the open road and made on average of one stop every two days. Using the truck, we interacted with 18 times more people than we could have reached via traditional mechanisms. We could interact with people in all roles, from C-level managers to engineers, makers, and students. We were even invited to bring the truck to a Maker Faire at the White House, which was hosted by President Obama. This resulted in headlines from the key media covering the event and positioned the company even more strongly at the heart of the Maker movement.

Having this truck gave us a different way of approaching the market. The truck provided a physical space to interact with people. The material presented in the truck amplified the message provided by our digital presence (on our website, social channels, community sites, etc.) on certain topics. When targeting new customers as part of an IoT campaign, we would first send targeted mail about the topic and then, for instance, target them through a dedicated LinkedIn campaign. Then, we would appear with the truck at their doors, serving lunch and providing their people with the opportunity to meet technical experts from our company face-to-face. In all this, we made sure that our message was consistent, whether we were at trade shows, in the truck, on our website and social channels, or engaging in face-to-face communication.

Figure 14: Exterior of the Atmel truck

Figure 15: Interior of the truck, as used for training

The truck worked on all the levels of marketing and branding. It was a traveling billboard for people to see (awareness); it contained demos so that people would get trained and become more strongly connected to the company (consideration and customer intimacy); and it exposed people to our roadmap and vision (long-term relationship-building through thought leadership and the boosting of brand loyalty). It served both the long

Figure 16: Atmel truck at the White House

tail and the key customers.

Additionally, some of our partners and distributors, were so happy with the truck that we sold them sponsorships on it. We partnered with distributors, as they have direct relationships with the customers. This way, we were working with the distributors to create demand such that the distributors could then go and fulfill the business. Hence, the truck created a win-win situation for the distributors and our company.

Instrument: Campaign approach

To run successful marketing campaigns that can reach people both digitally and physically, we apply a campaign process that consists of five phases. Throughout these phases, one person has ownership of and responsibility for the campaign; for large campaigns, a program manager is also involved. Campaign content is created for both online and offline channels (web pages, videos, brochures, sample kits, etc.), and it is designed to create a coherent, consistent message throughout the various touchpoints. All digital campaign content is tagged and measured to evaluate how effective it is so that we can learn from our successes and failures and steer campaigns as needed. Each campaign is evaluated after it has ended, and the resulting knowledge is shared within the multidisciplinary campaign team.

The stages and activities in the campaign process were as follows:

Step 1: Set the campaign objective.
- Define the campaign objective and key performance indicators (KPIs) in a briefing document.
- Get the business owner's or key account manager's agreement and a go or no-go on the campaign.

Step 2: Form and brief the team.
- Form the campaign team and core team.
- Create the value proposition.
- Create the main messaging and captured it in a detailed briefing document.

Step 3: Create the campaign.
- Conduct a kickoff session with the integrated campaign team.
- Detail the campaign and strategy.

- Begin campaign development and the production of deliverables.
- Engage in piloting.

Step 4: Roll out and improve the campaign.
- Execute the campaign.
- Monitor the results.
- Conduct campaign reporting based on the campaign KPIs.

Step 5: Evaluate and iterate.
- Finalize the campaign.
- Evaluate the campaign's results.
- Iterate by applying knowledge and using the gathered data (including customer profiles) to fine-tune the next campaign.

For an example of applying the approach see Nabben (2013).

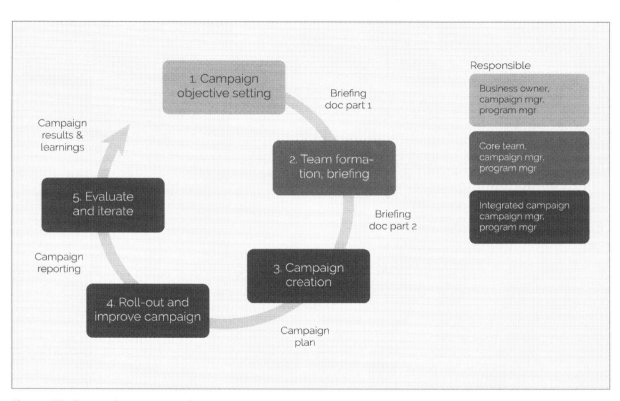

Figure 17: Campaign approach

Design for continuous change

Marketing operates in a world that is constantly changing: Your own offerings change, as do your competitors, and, most importantly, the people you target. Therefore, your engagement should be agile so that you can deal with this continuous change. To incorporate this agility in the DNA of our marketing organization, we apply a program approach. This approach combines two types of activities: Firstly, it includes activities for defining and regularly readjusting a vision. Secondly, it includes small improvement projects that take the organization in the right direction. As such, we combine long-term vision development with short-term results. This approach reflects the business reality, as constant changes require both a high level of agility and a continuous strategic direction.

The program approach creates agility and allows for uncertainty about where the organization should be in a couple of years, yet it still helps to take steps in the right direction.

In line with lean startup principles (Ries, 2011), we apply small experiments to validate assumptions about what the people who we are targeting need, and we steer initiatives in different directions if needed.

Mark
Geljon

The program approach helped us to incorporate change in our organization. We launched several tracks in parallel: Some were aimed at increasing the clarity of the vision, some dealt with innovation and experimentation, and others were meant to fix the fundamentals – the basics that we needed to make the vision a reality. This combination was great, as it helped to create clarity, but we could also take concrete steps, such as implementing a CMS system or improving the search feature.

What we learned is that this program approach is all about incorporating change in an organization in a very powerful way. It allowed us to organize ourselves, not only to redesign our website but also for our team's other activities. This way, we were able to deal with the constant changes in our organization. The program approach allowed us to embrace that constant change and organize ourselves toward it. We had groups working on specific improvement projects. In parallel, others were doing customer research to keep track of changing demands; we even had a group working on how to translate our vision into an improvement roadmap.

Supported by this structure, as a group, we were able to deal with the constant change that we were faced with: We constantly were asking for feedback and achieving improvements based on actual customer needs.

> All of this occurred while we were also being completely transparent and accountable for the activities we were executing. Stakeholders got peace of mind, which in turn resulted in the freedom to speed up and go for the intended results.

Instrument: Program approach

You should adopt the program approach in cases in which complexity and uncertainty do not allow for a project approach, such as when there is no clear point to work toward or no known route to get to that point. This approach combines four parallel activities:

1. Investigate the as-is situation: Where are we today? What customer groups do we serve? What are our products and services? How have we organized ourselves in terms of processes and functionality?

2. Create clarity on the vision: What is our vision? What activities would help to create a clearer vision? How can we translate that vision into an improvement roadmap?

3. Determine the boundaries: What restrictions in terms of budget, time, resources, and so forth must we deal with when defining improvement projects to achieve the vision? As with the other aspects, these boundaries change over time, so the program approach requires regularly reviewing the current boundaries.

4. Define improvement projects: What steps do you need to take to achieve specific goals? Note that these improvement projects

are to be managed with clear budgets and timelines. These projects bring you closer toward the vision, even though some specifics of the vision may not be known. These improvement project can be either quick wins or more fundamental improvements, as long as they have clear goals and processes that can be planned and managed to achieve those goals.

To help in defining and discussing the approach, the canvas by GriDD depicted in figure 18 can be used.

Conclusion

Designing for engagement is a creative process for which there is no fixed recipe for success. Nevertheless, there are three key ingredients to a successful marketing campaign. First, design for an optimized customer experience; armed with the customer insights you have gathered, create a user experience in which your customers are presented with the information they need in the format they need. Second, design for an integrated approach; be where your customers are, both in the digital world and in the physical world. Finally, design for continuous change. The world is in constant flux; therefore, your marketing campaign and marketing organization should be agile. Applying the program approach helps you to be agile and to create a continuous improvement cycle, through which you can focus on what really matters and cut the bullsh*t.

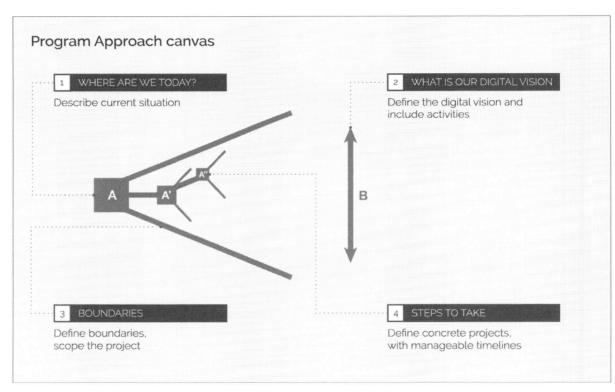

Program Approach canvas

1 WHERE ARE WE TODAY?
Describe current situation

2 WHAT IS OUR DIGITAL VISION
Define the digital vision and include activities

A · A' · A"

B

3 BOUNDARIES
Define boundaries, scope the project

4 STEPS TO TAKE
Define concrete projects, with manageable timelines

Figure 18: Program approach canvas – by GriDD

Create your own Cut the Bullsh*t marketing plan

11. How do we currently design for engagement, both physically and digitally?

You

12. How have we organized ourselves in terms of processes and functionality?

13. What key restrictions must we deal with?

Create your own Cut the Bullsh*t marketing plan

14. What activities can help to create a clearer vision?

You

15. Which short-term projects could bring us closer to the vision?

ENGAGE TO THE MAXIMUM! – TALES FROM THE FIELD

4

Cut the Bullsh*t Marketing is about creating value by doing rather than by talking about what to do. As soon as you know enough about the people you are targeting and have designed a plan for engagement, it is time for you to get out and start engaging with people. This chapter is all about that stage; this is the proof of the pudding – the moment when you will test your hypotheses about how your engagement will work and how it will add value for people.

In this chapter, we describe tales from the field rather than models. These are real examples that have been proven to work for us and that, hopefully, will inspire you to go out and experiment.

Doing, not talking!

Given that the "doing, not talking" attitude is central to Cut the Bullsh*t marketing, our first anecdote in this chapter is about just that. It is about letting people experience your product rather than talking about it and about engaging with them using a very personal approach.

Sander Arts explains this attitude:

Sander
Arts

People increasingly hate marketing. Today, everybody has self-publication power, and the consumer is more powerful than ever because he or she can tap into peers or social networks to get detailed information on any topic. When we started looking at Maker Faires for marketing purposes, we said that it was one thing to go out there and talk about our products in a corporate, traditional way and to describe how makers could use them in particular applications, but we decided to do it differently. Nobody wants to hear a corporate bullsh*t story. The Maker Faires are not the place for that! Thus, we built a booth that could feature individual makers:

actual people who were using our products in a variety of cool ways. Some of these people's creations were in the incubation or prototype stage, but others were a bit closer to the markets. However, that was the beauty of it, as there is a whole journey between incubating and having a product that is marketable. I call this "the journey from maker space to marketplace." Visitors to our booth could hear about that journey firsthand.

By giving real people a platform and illustrating the variety of stages of their journeys, we were able to engage in a personal and authentic way. Visitors could have a conversation with a real person who was using our real products and say, "Hey, how did you get started on this?" or "How did you solve this particular problem?"

The process of finding people to whom we could give a platform was also very personal: We picked people from the community with whom we had chemistry. It was more based on gut feel than on a rational decision-making process, but it always worked. We had, for instance, a 14-year-old boy who had built his own company based on our technology, as well as professional users who had created innovative products and launched crowd-funding campaigns that closed successfully, with significant investments.

Create a social footprint, even in a nonsocial community

Social media has significantly transformed the way marketing works; people-to-people marketing acknowledges the power of individuals and the role that social networks play in the decision-making process. Therefore, creating a social footprint for your brand, product, or marketing campaign is essential, even in domains that might not appear to be very social at first glance.

Jeroen Grit explains a successful experiment to create a social footprint:

Jeroen Grit

Many people think of the engineering community as being nonsocial. However, it is actually a very social community – just one that is very focused on a set of particular topics. The community is social in the way that members talk about hardware or software. There is no chitchat around it – no bullsh*t. Independent of its message, any marketing machine would often be considered chitchat or marketing fluff, simply by default. Our key goal was to provide people from the engineering community with something that would not be labeled as marketing fluff and that would really get their attention. We stayed close to their key interests, which in this community

meant hardware boards and technological innovations. Our new product was a 16-bit hardware board in a market in which a lot of people were still working with 8-bit boards[2] for their applications. Our plan was to create a larger market by providing new boards for their experiments. The assumption was that, from these experiments, they would gain a preference for the new technology, which would in turn influence their buying decisions at their jobs. As the organization was a major supplier of high-quality 16-bit solutions, its market – and thereby, its sales figures – would increase.

To get their attention, we combined two aspects by taking technological innovation and doing something special around it.

[2] An 8-bit board is a piece of hardware that allows engineers to experiment with a specific type of 8-bit microcontroller. The hardware provides the basics so that you can learn how to program the microcontroller, put your code on the board, and see how your code works.

We called the campaign "break your habit." In the campaign, we asked people to create videos of themselves destroying their old 8-bit boards in the most imaginative ways; if they shared their videos, they would receive new 16-bit boards in return. To get things started, we created a few example movies using sledgehammers and big machines to match this group's nerdy yet manly way of looking at content. The campaign went well. From our research, we knew that the target makers typically had a lot of these boards laying around, so the possibility of getting a new one for free by smashing an old one worked very well. People also took pride in coming up with the most creative ways to destroy their boards. We saw everything from big grinders, to Tesla coils, to thermite used to destroy the boards. As these people shared their movies within their networks, we got the exposure that we desired in the broader engineering community.

Bring the company to the customers

People-to-people marketing requires personal contact. In line with the philosophy of understanding the person you are targeting, it is important to be where your customer is; rather than relying on having the customer come to you at a trade show or large event, bring the company to the customers.

Sander
Arts

In our people-to-people approach, we were aiming at people who you can't necessarily talk to through a traditional sales organization. Traditional sales organizations are mostly wired to hunt elephants – the big companies – by going to these companies and closing deals, armed with the best technology their company can make and offering all the tech support that the customer needs. It's a very good model, and it is currently where most revenue comes from.

However, in addition to elephant hunting, we also aimed for a different target: the long tail of the business. We expected that, in the semiconductor sector, if we do business with a large group of small businesses, each of these businesses would provide limited revenue but as a group it would represent a higher total margin. We also believed that the small fish of today could become the large fish of tomorrow. Obviously, we realized that the traditional sales mechanisms could never work in this model; it is impossible to visit all these companies and customers using a traditional sales organization. Therefore, we decided to build a showcase for our products and to see whether we could bring that to the people.

The resulting solution, our truck, proved successful at reaching the smaller accounts that formed the long tail; we used it for various purposes, including hands-on technical trainings, 3D-printing demonstrations, and hackathons. It was fun because it allowed us to meet people who we would otherwise never have met. The serendipity associated with this is significant, and it takes believing in the concept for one to try. We needed that because, at first, it was hard to calculate the plan's ROI. Fortunately, I had a very supportive CEO and a sales organization that was extremely pleased with the fact that they could have a literal vehicle at their disposal so that they could pull up at the office of a customer or potential customer and showcase the entire company's technology portfolio.

Humanize the brand

When trying to reach people as a brand, you must realize that the people who you are trying to reach do not want to hear from marketing departments. The only way to reach your audience is through authentic people such as actual experts. This engagement can take many forms, including personal blogs on the company website, personal conversations, or online discussions with experts. In any case, successful people-to-people marketing is done by real people, who help to humanize the brand.

Sander
Arts

Technology only comes to life when people touch it. Then again, nobody wants to hear from the marketing department at a trade show saying, "Here is our latest chip, and you should use it, and it has the following features." Nobody wants to listen to that bullsh*t. Instead of putting our marketing department on stage, we identified a bunch of authentic people from within the company, such as technical people who would 3D-print things in their spare time or experiment at home with Arduino boards; these people were genuinely interested in the maker movement and were using the development boards themselves. That is who we would put out at the Maker Faires. These people used natural and authentic methods of engagement that were not based in selling. They did not say "You should go and buy this board." Instead, they said, "I 3D-printed something over the weekend, and I'm building this with it." From there, they would just have nice conversations.

For instance, a gentleman named Bob Martin worked for our company, and I used to call him "The Master Maker." I would introduce him to the audience by saying, "He's the Master Maker. If you want to have a real conversation with a real maker, don't come to me, as I'm just the head of marketing. He's Bob Martin, the Master Maker, and he'd love to talk to you about anything you're doing or to help you get to the next level on your project." I've never had the arrogance to think that people want to hear from marketing employees. We're just enablers and matchmakers if you think about it.

Make it fun!

One aspect of people-to-people engagement that should not be underestimated is fun. Conversations and work should both be fun, so good people-to-people marketing campaigns should be fun as well! We strongly believe in serendipity. Moreover, adding a sparkle to your campaigns is important, not just for the people you are targeting, but also for the employees within the marketing department, as having fun campaigns is great for internal employer branding.

Sander
Arts

One day, in my role as global head of marketing, I agreed with our genius Head of Social Engagement, Arthur Beavis, to have rap battles on social media with one of our distributors, Mouser Electronics. We discussed the idea with them and decided to start a rap. Thus, we started by sending this tweet: "We like 8 bits and we cannot lie. All you other makers can't deny," as a tongue-in-cheek version of the song "Baby Got Back." From there, Mouser Electronics stepped in, as planned, with "When a board drops in with 8 bit pins and a grounded interface you get sprung."

Then, to our surprise, the original singer, Sir Mix-a-Lot (Anthony Ray is his real name), started to participate. We decided to not miss a beat, literally, so we just continued the rap. Fortunately, I had informed my CEO of the original plan, as now – all of a sudden – we had something that was a little bigger than we had anticipated. It turns out that Sir Mix-a-Lot is a maker, an investor, and an electrical engineer; he built most of the equipment in his Seattle studios all by himself. We continued to engage with him because it was truly fun having somebody from outside of the industry participate. You can imagine the boost that it gave the brand but also the boost that it gave internally (from an employer-branding point of view) because everybody of a certain age here in the United States grew up with the song "Baby Got Back." Now, that guy was standing in the elevator at headquarters; people could take selfies with him and all of that, and he turned out to be a very approachable guy. I am still in touch with him.

You cannot plan for something like this; it is the kind of event that just happens. We decided to engage when it happened and to see where it would bring us. In the end, it was beneficial for both parties, and we created a lot of media attention with this campaign. The effort also got picked up by the mainstream media, who wrote about how a semiconductor company had started rapping with a rap artist.

Figure 19: Sander Arts and Sir Mix-a-Lot (Anthony Ray)

Tweets

Atmel Corporation @Atmel   1h
@MouserElec ♫ We like 8-bits and we cannot lie. All you other
Makers can't deny. ♫ #Atmel #TBT
Expand

Mouser Electronics @MouserElec   1h
@Atmel When a board drops in with 8 bit pins and a grounded
interface you get sprung. #tbt #Atmel @therealmix
View conversation

Sir Mix-A-Lot @therealmix   1h
@MouserElec @Atmel wanna pull up tough but your solder got
flow with flux
View conversation

Atmel Corporation @Atmel   1h
@therealmix @MouserElec ♫ Little in the middle with a shirt pin on
its back. ♫ #Atmel #TBT
View conversation

Mouser Electronics @MouserElec   1h
@Atmel @therealmix I'm tired of Double-E's saying 32-bits the thing.
#tbt #Atmel
View conversation

Garrett Mace @macegr   1h
@therealmix @MouserElec @Atmel Yeah baby, when it come to
uC's ARM got nothing to do with my selection. 72Mhz-256K? Only if
she's 8 bit.
View conversation

Atmel Corporation @Atmel   1h
@MouserElec @therealmix ♫ 'Cause our chips are small and
screen curves are kickin.' I'm thinkin' bout stickin'...with Atmel. ♫
#TBT
View conversation

Figure 20: Twitter conversation with Sir Mix-A-Lot

Conclusion

Cut the Bullsh*t marketing is about creating value by doing, experimenting, and testing to see what works. In this chapter, we shared a series of anecdotes about how we have engaged with customers. Three aspects are key to all these examples: engaging in personal interaction, being where the customer is (both digitally and physically), and making it fun. Cut the Bullsh*t marketing acknowledges that a professional setting is all about people-to-people interaction. This interaction should be fun. Such a marketing attitude requires a matching organization. Therefore, we will elaborate in the next chapter on the characteristics of a Cut the Bullsh*t marketing organization.

Create your own Cut the Bullsh*t marketing plan

16. How can you make it fun? Think outside of the box!

You

Create your own Cut the Bullsh*t marketing plan

Notes

You

CREATE A CUT THE BULLSH*T MARKETING ORGANIZATION

5

People-to-people, Cut the Bullsh*t marketing can only thrive in a matching organization. This chapter is about some of the organizational prerequisites. What does it take to create a Cut the Bullsh*t marketing organization? Above all, it takes drive, ambition, and willingness to take ownership. Successful marketing must be guided by a clear, bold marketing vision to ensure consistency across campaigns. The examples we have discussed in this book are best implemented using a flat marketing organization and properly aligned marketing functions. This chapter elaborates on these four organizational aspects.

Vision, ambition, drive, and ownership

Cut the Bullsh*t marketing is fueled by having a marketing **vision**, **ambition**, **drive**, and the willingness and ability to take **ownership**.

Marketing vision provides direction; it helps to focus the energy of a marketing team in a consistent direction. It is about the ability to think about future marketing with imagination and to see opportunities before the competition does.

Ambition is about having the willingness to do whatever it takes to achieve the vision. People often misread ambition as a blind desire for power, influence, or money. Fortunately, ambition can also be used toward more noble goals, such as offering the best service to a particular customer group or creating the best marketing team.

Effective marketers possess a drive to succeed that is contagious. They are able to motivate the people around them and to win these people over to their marketing vision. As every marketing organization faces challenges, this also requires a drive to succeed in the battles that undoubtedly will have to be fought along the way.

Ownership is a mind-set and an attitude. It is about taking responsibility for making sure that the intended result is happening. It is also about having the willingness to take responsibility when that result is not achieved. Leaders that take ownership empower high-performing teams to lead and win (Willink & Babin, 2015).

Vision, drive, ambition, and the willingness to take ownership are key traits in the personality of a Cut the Bullsh*t marketer.

Mark Geljon explains how these traits can help to create impact:

Mark
Geljon

As a team, working on a design, we did not allow ourselves to rest until we had really solved the case. We believed that we could create the best digital environment for engineers, and we were so ambitious and focused that we just did not stop. That drive could be seen in the personalities of all the team members. We had some startup spirit, and we wanted to show the rest of the company the impact that we could make as a digital team.

To achieve this, we took ownership of all the areas that we felt were crucial for delivering the best experience possible. For instance, another group produced the digital content. We aligned with them to discuss the overall vision and ask how we could support them in making the content even more effective for engineers. We also asked to be in the loop during the content-production process. The responsibility for creating outstanding content remained with that team, but we took ownership of the overall process. Similarly, technical support remained a separate function, but we aligned with that group to make sure that we could coordinate support for application engineers in the field, not as a second or third line of support but as part of the first line, to make sure that the application engineers had a consistent, good experience.

Have a clear, bold marketing vision to steer initiatives

Consistent people-to-people marketing must be guided by a clear, bold marketing vision. This shared vision helps to ensure consistency across campaigns. Moreover, it motivates people in the marketing department and helps to position that department in the broader organization. The Cut the Bullsh*t mentality requires clarity and boldness; although few people will contest the aspect of customer-centricity or the need to engage with customers in a personal way, the implications of engaging to the maximum might be startling. A bold statement helps to communicate marketing ambition not only to the rest of the organization but also to the people in the marketing department themselves.

Sander
Arts

When I started these marketing activities, we needed a clear, bold marketing vision so that the people in the organization could understand where this was going. Our company develops and sells semiconductors, but we had embraced a novel approach to marketing; for the organization, and especially the marketing department, to be truly different from the other semiconductor companies, the marketing department adopted a mindset in which we were going to build a media company that sells semiconductors.

The basis of this vision was that a successful semiconductor company requires a fan base, which is exactly what we were building. Through the media, we had helped startup companies go to market.

In the process, we had acquired such a large audience that we were able to help customers in their crowdfunding. We could steer a multitude of eyeballs toward interesting projects based on our technology. This helped in exposing the possibilities that our products offered and greatly increased our fan base. Yes, the marketing statement that we are a media company selling semiconductors was bold, but such bold statements are needed to reach ambitious goals and create coherence in marketing initiatives.

None of our competitors could offer this type of differentiation. It turned out to be very distinctive. Let me explain. Many startups (especially those in IoT) create a prototype using an Arduino development board. That board contains an Atmel microcontroller. To get funding, many entrepreneurs choose a crowdfunding site (Indiegogo, Crowdsupply, and Kickstarter, to name a few). Whenever a campaign was launched, if the technology was powered by Atmel, we would make sure to give it attention on all our channels and blogs. That way, we created a gigantic audience, making the results even more fun. Entrepreneurs would turn to us and enthusiastically tell us that they had reached their projects' crowdfunding goals quickly. They all saw large jumps in support from their backers after we wrote about their projects on our channels. In brief, we were able to channel so many eyeballs to these campaign pages that funding became easier. No other semiconductor company could compete with that; they had to see

customers swap out their solutions for Atmel versions because we gave the entrepreneurs love and attention on our channels, thus making them wildly successful.

Create a flat, coherent marketing organization

To create successful Cut the Bullsh*t marketing, it is essential that KPIs are set to align with the organization's strategy and business goals. KPIs need to be formulated in such a way that everyone in the organization (including those outside of the marketing department) knows how they, as individuals, are responsible for contributing to these KPIs.

In traditional marketing organizations, individuals have KPIs for their own individual disciplines, which often leads to suboptimal results. Let's take public relations (PR) as an example. PR managers are held responsible for putting out press releases and for ensuring there are press briefings and press coverage. The effectiveness of these press releases and their contributions to the campaigns' success are often not part of PR managers' KPIs.

In contrast, if KPIs are defined based on business priorities and aligned with those priorities, the PR manager will also be held accountable for the campaigns' results. The PR manager thus also has goals that are seemingly outside of PR. How can that person influence sales figures, you may ask? Well, the PR manager now has to "lean in" and become a true sparring partner of the campaign team. The manager has to figure out how to support the creation of both more technical content and more

relevant content for the campaign pages, the social engagement, and the dedicated pieces of advertising. All of this triggers more collaboration, discussion, and teamwork.

Shared goals help a lot in driving toward achieving the optimal culture, collaboration, and results, whether for a team or the entire company. Shared goals also eliminate the bullsh*t because they provide a laser-sharp focus on the task at hand and on the results that need to be accomplished.

KPIs must reflect business priorities, and they should be formulated to be Specific, Measurable, Attainable, Relevant, and Time-bound (or SMART). Indicators that should be included in KPI descriptions are, for instance, the number of visitors to the landing pages, the number of people downloading certain key assets (such as white papers, application notes, and reference designs), the number of evaluation kits or development boards shipped, the number of qualified leads, the customer count, the identified sales potential, and sales figures. KPIs should be dependent on the maturity of the marketing organization (including its capability of measuring results).

Marketing employees need to work together as a coherent group, and, most importantly, they have to create an effective, consistent message for the customers. Having a flat organization helps to achieve this, as it improves the flow of information within the organization by breaking down the silos that typically form when there is too much middle management. With the focus on customers and on people-to-people marketing, a flat marketing organization rotates the traditional organizational chart. With

such an organization, it is more logical to talk about customer-facing frontline employees and a back office that supports these troops. This transformed view helps to create a more consistent customer experience, as the frontline employees, who are closer to the customer than anyone else, work together as a coherent group, without the artificial boundaries that exist when these people report to different middle managers.

Sander
Arts

Many marketing organizations are still rooted in old-school behavior. This stems from the fact that, in the past, marketing organizations were mainly doing public relations, corporate communications, events, branding, and advertising. The effects of these behaviors are typically hard to measure, but such areas are where the bulk of the marketing budgets are going. With the current digital transformation, and with marketing automation and digital tracking of customer behavior, there is an increasing amount of data available for analysis. Armed with insights based on this data, we can talk about the ROI of marketing campaigns and the results of lead-nurturing activities – not just in terms of impressions but in terms of leads and revenue.

That's how organizations must change; we need to break down the silos that stop truly integrated approaches. This means that, instead of focusing on separate activities related to public relations, corporate communication, branding, and advertising, people in the marketing department need to collaborate on a campaign or engagement process – and be measured as such.

If layers are created in an organization, or if such layers are kept in place, information will not flow very well through the organization. This is because everybody remains focused on their own silos, which is not the recipe for success on a campaign level. Therefore, I flattened the marketing organization. At the same time,

I made individuals responsible for the impact of each campaign, in whatever shape or form. We defined the KPIs associated with each cam-paign outcome rather than with the tasks that individuals or groups have to perform: It is not about what you do or (even worse) how much time you spend – it is about the outcome! This has profound consequences for the rest of the organization, but it needs to be done.

As summarized in Figure 21, integrated campaigns require functional areas in which they can work together to reach the customer with a coherent, consistent message. Therefore, these groups should not have unrelated KPIs; instead, they should have a set of campaigns that combines their individual KPIs and the KPIs associated with the campaign outcome.

Create an end-to-end marketing campaign process

Throughout this book, we have described how people-to-people marketing campaigns generate ROI in the form of revenue or identified sales potential. Successfully creating and running such campaigns requires good teams, with a variety of competencies, both from within the marketing department and from the rest of the organization. To guide such teams, and to make sure a successful marketing campaign is not a one-off, team members need clear, shared end-to-end campaign processes. All those involved need to understand and follow these processes. The approach should give direction, help to make sure all the essential steps are taken, and help people focus on what is important. In larger organizations, this method combines the strengths of

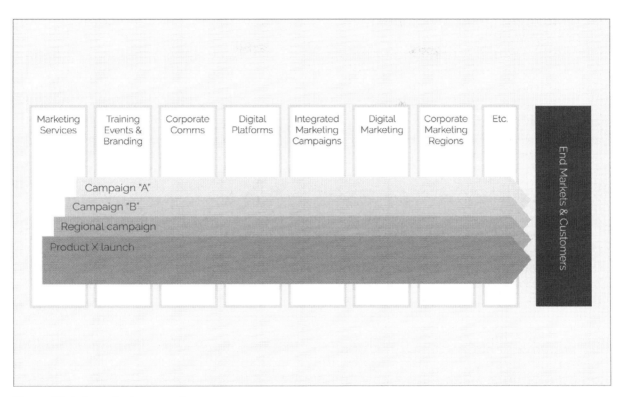

Figure 21: Integrated campaigns

119

the centralized and decentralized parts of the organization. Typically, enabling, quality control, and steering toward consistency should be the responsibility of the core organization; the decentralized parts of the organization typically have much clearer views of the customers and the local markets.

Mark
Geljon

To be successful on the larger campaigns, we needed to tackle them in an integral way. Therefore, we introduced an end-to-end campaign process involving all the various marketing functions; we integrated everything: direct marketing, email marketing, digital activities, and even events. It was quite a difficult process, involving a large number of stakeholders and external experts, but it made a big difference. The results showed

the importance of approaching marketing activities from an integral point of view.

When we started, the various marketing areas already had their own processes, so we had to convince them to change their ways of working. We did so from not only functional but also centralized and decentralized perspectives; we involved all business lines and markets so that marketers from specific business lines in specific locations would start work together with the core marketing staff as colleagues, as they should, to achieve campaign results.

In the end-to-end process, we acknowledged that the decentralized groups had better knowledge of their customers. In all digital activities, we tried to balance the business needs of the local business lines and the facilities that the core organization could provide to promote consistency. The decentralized groups could easily go to their own vendors to create their own websites or campaign materials, so we had to fulfill their needs in a good way; otherwise, they would just create materials themselves.

Work with Cut the Bullsh*t business partners

To create a successful Cut the Bullsh*t marketing campaign, it is essential to work in an ecosystem of business partners who also follow the Cut the Bullsh*t philosophy. If you work with external partners, such as for graphic design, website development, or marketing asset development, these partners must have a deep willingness to understand the people who you are targeting; they must also use an appropriate tone of voice, be able to work at your level of pragmatism and agility, and challenge others (including you!) when bullsh*t is introduced.

Working in an ecosystem of Cut the Bullsh*t business partners places requirements on the way you work together:

• Be clear about the **strengths**, **weaknesses**, **roles**, and **responsibilities** of all partners in the network. Make sure that the parties in the ecosystem can work together without mediation and orchestration of each activity.

- **Share customer insights** to ensure that everyone is on the same page about the people you are targeting; share persona descriptions and information about the customers' journeys.

- Work together as **partners**, not like a client working with suppliers (as in the traditional model). By making your business partners part of your team, you can achieve through-sourcing: instead of insourcing people or outsourcing activities to external agencies, in this model, your marketing team can learn from your business partners, and your partners can better understand your context and priorities.

- All the partners in the ecosystem must **take ownership** for the parts they are responsible for. Although scoping responsibilities is important, partners must have the attitude that they will deliver what is needed, with the right quality, and within the agreed-upon time and budget constraints.

In our case, the success of everything we did was a result of the commitment and dedication of all parties involved: from the freelance project manager to the marcom lady in a small sales office abroad and from the big IT supplier to the consultancy boutique supplying great models. We do not want to imply that we created everything or took all the responsibility. What we did do is create the conditions and drive that allowed everyone to be involved and to succeed in making marketing work!

Conclusion

A Cut the Bullsh*t marketing organization requires four key elements: a clear, bold marketing vision; the ambition to excel; a drive to deliver, no matter what; and a leader who takes ownership. In our experience, this works best in a flat marketing organization, in which people do not hide in hierarchies but instead share commitments and responsibilities. The same holds for the external partners you work with; these partners should also have a Cut the Bullsh*t attitude and should take ownership and be able to work with the same level of agility. When these elements are in place, you can create an effective end-to-end marketing campaign process that will have an impact, as we will discuss in the next chapter.

Create your own Cut the Bullsh*t marketing plan

17. Who are your Cut the Bullsh*t marketing partners?
How can you ensure that they succeed?

You

18. What is the level of marketing knowledge in your organization?

Create your own Cut the Bullsh*t marketing plan

19. Describe your bold marketing vision in no more than 200 words.

You

THE IMPACT OF CUT THE BULLSH*T MARKETING

6

When marketing budgets are under pressure, and time is a scarce resource, marketing campaigns must have a positive ROI, and marketing leaders must have the ability to show how the money spent in the marketing budget contributed to the bottom line. The only way to receive more budget from a CEO or CFO is to generate revenue through marketing activities. Cut the Bullsh*t marketing is no different. In this chapter, we show the impact of Cut the Bullsh*t marketing, based on our own experience of applying this approach.

Return on investment and revenue

Whereas marketing departments may see the impact of winning a marketing award or of increased media exposure, at the end of the day, the real impact of marketing must also be measurable in terms of ROI and revenue. In our experience, Cut the Bullsh*t marketing has helped to establish significant results.

Sander Arts provides the Atmel case as an example:

Sander
Arts

At the end of 2012, when I joined the company, Atmel was rich in products and supporting content, but as with the industry in general, it was struggling with slowing demand and tight profit margins. Recognizing that the spoils go to the nimble, we set out on a course to turn Atmel's knowledge of the buyer's journey into a competitive advantage. In the process, we turned a traditional marketing organization – which was siloed and service/support-oriented – into a sales enabler that was accountable for both ROI and revenue. My goal from the start has been to improve Atmel's marketing from good to great and to deliver revenue through the marketing organization.

In the Atmel case, the impact of the Cut the Bullsh*t marketing approach has paid off on several fronts.

Sales: The sales force is actively following up on leads that are generated through global, integrated marketing campaigns. In addition, the global key account managers are excited about the data and analysis that we can provide about their key customer base. We look at the data analytics generated from website behavior and use it in the day-to-day sales process. In the last couple of years, various marketing-engagement programs have more than doubled the number of prospective leads in our marketing database. Sales are engaged to the point at which key account managers are starting to request new marketing campaigns that target specific audiences and products. This is cool because it involves doing marketing with your sales people, when normally you would only be doing marketing with marketing people. We are reaching the point at which the boundary between sales and marketing will disappear.

Metrics: These days, marketing involves measuring everything. We have set up large monitors at our headquarters to serve as a giant dashboard to track both traditional metrics (such as page views, retweets, and likes) and real KPIs relating to revenue and ROI. Overall, the campaigns have generated $50 in sales opportunities for every dollar spent. Some campaigns have outperformed that number significantly, generating as much as $2,500 in sales opportunities for every dollar spent. To gain these insights, we have tracked and analyzed results from all our marketing campaigns, comparing the results from before and after the campaign launch. We track results throughout all the stages of the buyer's journey – including awareness, several conversion points, and, of course, sales. Behind the scenes, we measure many indicators, including visits to the website; changes in product page views; increases in the number of leads, scored for sales potential; generated sales potential; and download rates for data sheets, application notes, and all documents.

Social: The marketing department has become very attuned to social media and is networking with the semiconductor community. Although we can't control the message, we can be on top of what's going on and participate in the conversations. We can be involved, and that is what is happening. Atmel was ranked by Publitek as the most social semiconductor company in September 2014 and is still the #1 most-viewed partner on ARM's connected community.

Culture: Atmel Academy, an internal training group, is helping everyone in the company to become media savvy. It is training employees in the many elements of digital marketing, such as how to conduct successful webinars, how to make videos, how to blog, and how to engage customers and prospects via social media.

Corporate: The CEO and the board are most interested in knowing the number of qualified leads coming in, the ratio of sales to leads, the increases in downloads of evaluation kits and product samples, and the increases in sales. They want to know how we are increasing conversions and how those conversions are resulting in more revenue. They want the story of our results in the form of revenue. One result that we have already seen is that a 1% increase in qualified leads can lead to an additional $1 million in revenue, even with all other aspects (e.g., sales accepted, sales qualified, and percentage of wins) remaining the same.

At the end of the day, everything still comes down to the bottom line: revenue and ROI. It was essential to show that the marketing approach yields positive results and that the campaigns generated up to $2,500 in sales opportunities for every marketing dollar spent.

In the last few years, at various companies, our Cut the Bullsh*t approach has created significant results and impact. The market has rewarded the teams with a long list of impressive marketing awards.

Sander
Arts

Earlier in my career, I noticed that when the management team saw the marketing team on stage accepting awards and celebrating, the managers were sometimes annoyed. They were living in the dark ages and fighting their own battles. They had no idea that our hard work and dedication had resulted in more customers and more sales for them. They could not see beyond our celebrations. For me, this was an important lesson in being clear about the ROI and impact of successful marketing.

Six essential ingredients for measuring marketing campaign impact

To establish a seat at the table for strategic discussions in the boardroom, marketing will have to be able to show how it contributes to ROI and revenue. The foundation for this is being able to measure marketing impact. The following six ingredients are essential in measuring marketing campaign impact:

1. Have one person responsible for each marketing campaign: setting the objectives, creating content, supporting activation, measuring results, all the way to ending the campaign.
2. Define a SMART goal for each marketing campaign; it should be specific, measurable, assignable, realistic, and time-related. Align these goals with those of

the organization and state how the campaign will contribute to them.

3. Measure a campaign's results in terms of its contribution to revenue and ROI. For instance, track how the campaign contributes to sales (or sales potential).

4. Tag and track all campaign content to measure how effective that content is. Adapt it if needed based on the results that come back in during the campaign;

5. Create tailored campaign-related dashboards showing the progress toward the campaign goals. Tailor these dashboards to the different groups so that each group gets its relevant information at the appropriate level of detail. A campaign dashboard for a marketing leadership meeting is different from a dashboard for the content team. The information must be available in the same rhythm that the teams work in.

6. Have regular, short meetings with the multidisciplinary campaign team to review campaign effectiveness, to extract knowledge and good ractices, and to steer campaigns as needed.

Recognition of the approach

The Cut the Bullsh*t marketing approach has received a broad range of recognition, including:

2015:
- Winner, ACE Award, B2B Account-Based Marketing Excellence. (http://www.prnewswire.com/news-releases/demandbase-announces-winners-of-inaugural-demandbase-ace-awards-300074937.html);
- Winner, Exhibitor Magazine's All-Star Award for Atmel's Road Map;
- Winner, WEB Award, B2B Standard of Excellence for the Philips Lighting .com

redesign;
- Runner-up, Markie Award, Modern Marketing Leader of the Year;
- Finalist, Supernova Award for Digital Marketing Transformation;
- Approach used in Stanford Graduate School of Business training (Shiv & Hoyt, 2015).

2014:
- Winner, Exhibitor All-Star Marketing Award for the Atmel mobile trailer;
- Winner, Publitek: semiconductor companies winning in social media;
- Short-listed, Markie Award, Most Creative Marketing Campaign, for the Atmel AVR contest.

2012:
- Winner, Integrated Marketing Award for Microcontroller Central. (http://www.minonline.com/awards/ima2012_finalists/);
- Winner, Web Marketing Association's

annual WebAward (http://www.webaward.org/winner.asp?eid=18621), Outstanding Achievement in Web Development, for Microcontroller Central (http://www.microcontroller central.com/).

2011:
- Winner, EMMA Award, Best Mobile App for a visionary mobile marketing roadmap in the B2B area;
- Finalist, World Wide B2B Marketing Awards (Mobile at the Fingertips of Engineers) for NXP's mobile app;
- Winner, WEB Award for Outstanding Achievement in Web Marketing;
- Winner, Sabre Award for the European E-call campaign (with NXP, BMW, and partners);
- Winner, IPRA Award for the European E-call campaign (with NXP, BMW, and partners);
- Winner, European Excellence Award for the European E-call campaign (with

NXP, BMW, and partners);

- Top 100 Marketers list, Marketing Magazine (The Netherlands);
- Top 10 Most Influential International RFID Brands in China, International Internet of Things Technologies & Applications Association (http://goo.gl/6fWAE);
- Named one of the Most Popular Semiconductor Brands in China, China Electronic News, one of the most influential electronics/semiconductor publications in China (http://goo.gl/apllF);
- Finalist, Electronics Choice Industry Awards for Marketing Excellence, Best Digital Marketing e-Campaign, for the Microcontrollers Cortex-M0 Integrated Marketing Campaign. (http://www.eciaonline.org/documents/ECIAMarketingAwards2011 Winners.pdf).

2010:
- Winner, OMMA Award, Business-to Business Integrated Online Campaigns;
- Winner, WEB Award, Outstanding Achievement in Web Marketing;
- Winner, WEB Award, B2B Standard of Excellence;
- Determined positioning and marketing for NXP's IPO on August 6, 2010 – one of the largest IPOs of that year;
- Finalist, B2B Marketing Awards, Best Lead Generation Campaign, for "Join the Lighting Revolution";
- Launched NXP's redesigned website, which is truly community-built, and which won the B2B Standard of Excellence Web Award for Outstanding Achievement in Web Development; the site also improved conversion by 300%+.

Conclusion

Although page views and downloads are easy to measure, the real KPIs of marketing must be related to the revenue and impact that it creates. It is key to determine the results that marketing has to create and how you are going to measure them.

These days, almost everything can be tracked, including the geographical origin of digital traffic, the number of calls to the service desk, the amount of product sales in a specific region, and the number of people who have scanned a QR code on a campaign booth and subsequently placed an order. Although all this information can be gathered, you should not treat all data equally. It is essential to focus on the indicators that are closely related to the organization's strategic direction. Cut the bullsh*t and limit yourself only to reports on performance indicators that are truly key. When you observe interesting patterns, you may need to have data analysts dig deeper into the underlying details to uncover the "why." Your tasks are to translate those insights into experiences for marketing and to improve ROI and revenue.

Create your own Cut the Bullsh*t marketing plan

20. What is the intended result of your marketing?

You

21. How are you going to measure the results of your marketing?

Create your own Cut the Bullsh*t marketing plan

22. Describe your marketing dream: What is your ultimate goal? How will you know when you have attained that goal?

You

AFTERWORD

Will today's CMO still be relevant in three years? By then, will the CMO still have a seat at the table for key strategic decisions? To stay relevant, the CMO needs to have a clear marketing vision, plus ambition, drive, and the willingness to take ownership for marketing results. The CMO needs to be able to show how the marketing team contributed to the bottom line and how the money spent in the marketing budget generated dollars in sales opportunities. This holds both for B2C and B2B settings, as both revolve around actual people who influence and make decisions.

In this book, we have shown that marketing is all about people-to-people engagement in what is traditionally called a B2B setting. Whether you are targeting known key customers or the masses in the long tail, the personal marketing approach yields the biggest returns. As documented in the Stanford case (Shiv & Hoyt, 2015),

93% of B2B purchases start with an Internet search, and 70% of the buying process is complete before prospects engage with a live salesperson (Neeson and Reap, 2012).

This all points to the need for a personal, authentic marketing approach that uses the full potential of digital channels and social media. Only then will the marketing stay relevant, allowing the CMO to have a seat at the table while delivering ROI and revenue.

The road ahead: Artificially intelligent personalized marketing

Recent advances have paved the way for artificially intelligent support in personalized marketing. Given the current possibilities of tracking customers across digital and physical environments, marketing departments have become equipped with (big) data sets that allow them to provide targeted content to match each customer's current context.

At the same time, artificial intelligence (AI) is rapidly advancing, as are its uses in business settings. Today, AI chat bots can already handle frequently asked questions in customer contact centers, only handing over the most complex questions to human agents. Similarly, AI assistants can schedule meetings for you and interact with your contacts via email using a human tone of voice (see, for instance, http://x.ai).

Such AI agents, armed with rich data sets, will soon be able to provide personalized marketing in a way that creates the illusion of interacting with a human being. This will allow for much more tailored marketing that focuses on the needs of individuals. We will see marketing solutions tailoring content not just to groups such as civil engineers, but to particular people, such as civil engineers who happen to be IoT enthusiasts as well. Key to this will be striking a balance between providing customer value through relevant, tailored content and respecting the privacy of the individual customers. After all, customers may be put off by a feeling of being observed by a company (as with "Big Brother").

Although AI is developing quickly, smart humans will be the ones to create the scripts, craft the messages, come up with creative campaigns, and design engagements with other people. Hence, the personal factor that we describe in this book remains important, even if some of the campaigns are executed by AI agents.

Cut the bullsh*t!

With our Cut the Bullsh*t approach, marketing really can add ROI and revenue. For example, for every dollar spent on the campaigns mentioned in this book, we have generated $50 in sales opportunities. Some campaigns have even generated as much as $2,500 in sales opportunities for every dollar spent. We strongly believe that this can be done for any brand and any business. There are no unglamorous products – only unimaginative solutions. Every product has key value propositions and/or features that can be leveraged. There are communities everywhere; there is always engagement potential; and there is always an opportunity to humanize the brand. Remember: *products are created in factories, but brands are created in the mind.*

The key takeaway of this book is that, for your people-to-people marketing activity to be successful, you need to understand your customer. It is important to execute campaigns in an orderly fashion and to keep the team focused on what matters most: results in the form of revenue.

We should not forget to cut the bullsh*t ourselves. The quick reader would argue that we are also putting up a lot of bullsh*t and that we are selling marketing methods instead of raw earnings. Remember the crucial difference: bullsh*t is when marketing is presented as a deliverable – a result in itself. It should always be positioned as a means to an end – a way to create loyal customers and add revenue. How, though, can you recognize bullsh*t marketing?

Bullsh*t marketing	Cut the Bullsh*t marketing
Refers to customer segments	Refers to personas
Presents marketing models as solutions	Presents marketing models as a means to an end
Oversimplifies the domain	Embraces the complexity of the domain
Learns what customers need from sales	Learns what customers need from the customers themselves
Is at the wrong place at the wrong time	Is where the customer is at the relevant moments
Has a one-dimensional view of customers	Understands that customers are multifaceted
Designs complex solutions	Designs an elegant solution
Talks in a corporate voice	Talks in a human, personal voice
Is unimaginative	Makes marketing fun!
Works in perfect isolation	Aligns with the business, the CEO/CFO, and the board of directors
Creates a hierarchical marketing organization	Creates a flat marketing organization

Bullsh*t marketing	Cut the Bullsh*t marketing
Has a strong boundary between the marketing department and external agencies	Builds a strong team, including specialists from external agencies
Reports about conversion rates and page views	Reports about happy customers and revenue
Adds bullsh*t!	Adds revenue and ROI!

We therefore end with one more message: The only way to achieve real marketing results is to cut the bullsh*t, go out there, and experiment!

REFERENCES

ANDERSON, C. (2006). THE LONG TAIL: WHY THE FUTURE OF BUSINESS IS SELLING LESS OF MORE. HYPERION BOOKS. ISBN 1401302378

ARTS, S. (2016). FROM MAKERSPACE TO MARKETPLACE: UNLIMITED POSSIBILITIES TO CHANGE THE WORLD. WHITE PAPER. PUBLISHED AT NEWELECTRONICS: HTTP:// WWW.NEWELECTRONICS.CO.UK

DEMANDBASE (2017). ATMEL BOOSTS SALES OPPORTUNITIES 156% IN VARIOUS MARKET SEGMENTS WITH WEB PERSONALIZATION FOR KEY VERTICALS. https://www.demandbase.com/case-study/atmel-boosts-sales-opportunities-156/

GRAY, D., BROWN, S., MACANUFO, J. (2010). GAMESTORMING: A PLAYBOOK FOR INNOVATORS, RULEBREAKERS, AND CHANGEMAKERS. O'REILLY MEDIA, INC.

GRIDD (2016A). CUSTOMER ACTIVITY CYCLE CANVAS. GRIDD EFFECTIVE INFORMATION, THE NETHERLANDS. HTTP:// WWW.CUTTHEBULLSHITMARKETING.COM/ TOOLKIT

GRIDD (2016B). EFFECTIVE STORY MAP. GRIDD EFFECTIVE INFORMATION, THE NETHERLANDS. HTTP:// WWW. CUTTHEBULLSHITMARKETING.COM/TOOLKIT

GRIDD (2016C). PERSONA CANVAS. GRIDD EFFECTIVE INFORMATION, THE NETHERLANDS. HTTP:// WWW. CUTTHEBULLSHITMARKETING.COM/TOOLKIT

GRIDD (2016D). PROGRAM APPROACH CANVAS. GRIDD EFFECTIVE INFORMATION, THE NETHERLANDS. HTTP:// WWW. CUTTHEBULLSHITMARKETING.COM/TOOLKIT

GRIDD (2016E). UX CONCEPT APPROACH. GRIDD EFFECTIVE INFORMATION, THE NETHERLANDS. HTTP:// WWW. CUTTHEBULLSHITMARKETING.COM/TOOLKIT

GRIT, J. (2011). XLS EXIT: COLLABORATING ON REQUIREMENTS USING MINDMAP CONCEPTS. EUROIA POSTER. EUROIA, PRAGUE, CZECH REPUBLIC. DOWNLOADED FROM: http://lanyrd.com/2011/euroia/shhpk/

HIDALGO, C. (2011). DITCH B2B AND THINK B2P (BUSINESS TO PEOPLE), MARKETINGPROFS. http://www.marketingprofs.com/opinions/2011/23358/ditch-b2b-and-think-b2p-business-to-people

KRISHNAMURTHY, S. (2001). PERSON-TO-PERSON MARKETING: THE EMERGENCE OF THE NEW CONSUMER WEB, WASHINGTON UNIVERSITY. http://faculty.washington.edu/sandeep/d/p2pqjec.pdf

LEVINE, R., LOCKE, C., SEARLS, D.; WEINBERGER, D. (2000). THE CLUETRAIN MANIFESTO: THE END OF BUSINESS AS USUAL. CAMBRIDGE, MA: PERSEUS. ISBN 0738204315.

NABBEN, H. (2013). INTEGRATED MARKETING FOR INTEGRATED CIRCUITS. HTTPS://BLOG.NXP.COM/INNOVATION/INTEGRATED-MARKETING-FOR-INTEGRATED-CIRCUITS

NEESON J., REAP, M. (2012). MARKETING ORGANIZATION: NEXT FIVE YEARS. SIRIUSDECISIONS.

NEWMAN, D. (2014). HOW PERSONAL EMOTIONS FUEL B2B PURCHASES, FORBES. DOWNLOADED FROM: http://www.forbes.com/sites/danielnewman/2014/05/07/how-personal-emotions-fuel-b2b-purchases/

OSTERWALDER, A., PIGNEUR, Y., BERNARDA, G., SMITH, A., PAPADAKOS, T. (2014). VALUE PROPOSITION DESIGN: HOW TO CREATE PRODUCTS AND SERVICES

CUSTOMERS WANT. WILEY & SONS. ISBN: 978-1-118-96805-5.

RIES, E. (2011). THE LEAN STARTUP: HOW TODAY'S ENTREPRENEURS USE CONTINUOUS INNOVATION TO CREATE RADICALLY SUCCESSFUL BUSINESSES.

SHIV, B., HOYT, D. (2015) ATMEL: IGNITING THE B2C IN B2B. STANFORD UNIVERSITY TEACHING NOTE GSB NO. M-360, STANFORD UNIVERSITY.

SORRELLS, A. (2013). FORGET B2B AND B2C – TECH ENABLES B2P (BUSINESS TO PEOPLE) MARKETING, ORACLE. DOWNLOADED FROM: https://blogs.oracle.com/socialspotlight/forget-b2b-and-b2c-tech-enables-b2p-business-to-people-marketing

STRATEGYZER AG (2017). VALUE PROPOSITION CANVAS, ZÜRICH, SWITZERLAND. DOWNLOADED FROM https://strategyzer.com/canvas/value-proposition-canvas. USED WITH PERMISSION OF STRATEGYZER AG.

VANDERMERWE, S. (2000). HOW INCREASING VALUE TO CUSTOMERS IMPROVES BUSINESS RESULTS, MIT SLOAN MANAGEMENT REVIEW, VOL 42., PP. 27-34.

WILLINK, J., BABIN, L. (2015). EXTREME OWNERSHIP: HOW U.S. NAVY SEALS LEAD AND WIN. ST. MARTIN'S PRESS., NEW YORK. ISBN 978-1-250-06705-0.

ABOUT THE AUTHORS

Sander Arts, MS, was born in the Netherlands. He is a true global citizen who is currently living and working in the heart of Silicon Valley. He is an award-winning Global Head of Marketing, strategic advisor, board member, and lecturer who has extensive experience in increasing revenue and meaningfully reaching (technical) audiences that were historically considered not to care about marketing – hardware and software engineers. As the former Global Head of Marketing of Atmel Corporation and the Global Head of Brand and Marketing at Philips and NXP Semiconductors, Sander transformed the company's marketing organization, while guiding the global teams to successfully implement a people-to-people lead generation campaign strategy. In the various organizations he has worked for, Sander has passionately promoted in-depth research into customer behavior, creating personas, and understanding the customers' journey. He holds a master's degree from Nijmegen University, and a certificate in strategic marketing management from the executive program at Stanford Graduate School of Business. He lectures in Stanford's Strategic Marketing Program. He is the founder of his own strategic marketing consultancy, Orange Tulip, LLC, in Silicon Valley. He is known for his direct, "no-bullsh*t" approach, building global high-performing teams, generating results that matter, his pragmatism, and his "can-do" spirit.

Mark Geljon, MS, is managing partner and founder of GriDD. Since 2000 he is creating effective organizations by designing information concepts, creating understandable strategies, and encouraging employees and executives to pursue ambitious visionary goals. Using the methodologies of information architecture and his entrepreneurial pragmatism, he boosts companies into effective human-centered revenue machines. Always at the forefront of new developments, Mark is one of initiators of the visual thinking community in the Netherlands and is currently working to develop the new field of story architecture and proposition building. As a principal consultant for multinational corporations and a coach to executives, entrepreneurs, and TEDx speakers, Mark is known for his ability to facilitate bottom line impact. Furthermore, he is an expert on story architecture, and he knows how to connect with people, create impact, and initiate change. His extensive experience in the high tech and engineering industry has proven to be essential in setting up impactful transformation programs and change initiatives, both in corporate as startup environments. Mark has worked as consultant and manager for a large number of multinational B2B companies, including Philips, NXP, Royal Haskoning DHV, and Teijin Aramid. As a passionate maker, he knows how to craft the ultimate revenue engine. Mark holds a master's degree in Systems Engineering, Policy Analysis, and Management from Delft University of Technology.

Jeroen Grit, MS, is managing partner and user experience lead at GriDD. As an experienced strategist, he excels in creating the digital infrastructure and underlying "plumbing" necessary to fulfill ambitious marketing strategies that reach customers and generate sales results. As an experienced behavioral science professional and passionate UX strategist and designer, he knows how to craft the ideal machinery, both technical as organizational, for delivering a top-class customer experience. Jeroen thoroughly understands that every B2B environment has its specific challenges, and he is very experienced in reducing complexity so that generic design principles can be applied to bring the performance to the next level. His background in communication science and his research experience in the area of new media research and design, combined with his passionate and energetic attitude, has proven to be an indispensable asset for many large global marketing change programs. Jeroen has worked for companies such as Royal Philips, Philips Lighting, NXP, Atmel, Marvell, Pentair, and Twente University. As a former speed biking champion, he knows what is necessary to win. Jeroen holds a master's degree from Twente University.

About the editor

Robert Slagter, PhD, MS, is principal consultant at GriDD and active practitioner of the Cut the Bullsh*t methodologies. He advises and guides large organizations by bringing structure to complex settings, while focusing on clients and employees. He has a passion for understanding what information people need to be effective and how organizations and technology can be designed to support this. Robert has over 15 years of experience in creating impact in high tech, financial, and government organizations. His publications include journal articles and books on designing systems for remote collaboration and on information maturity in organizations. His background in enterprise architecture and information ergonomics have proven to be the secret ingredient for successful global change initiatives in multiple markets. As an active bushcrafter, he knows how to get the most out of every business situation and survive the most extreme situations. He received a PhD from Twente University based on his research into systems that help global teams work together effectively, even if their way of working changes over time.

Orange Tulip Consultancy, LLC

Orange Tulip is a strategic consultancy firm based in the heart of Silicon Valley, California. It services a variety of global clients in the B2B and B2C space. Orange Tulip operates in the IoT (Internet of Things), automotive, distribution, consulting, start-up, media, education, hardware, software, E-commerce, and the technology and innovation space.

Customers do business with Orange Tulip because they have a need for (Interim) CMO work, strategic marketing, strategic advice, digital transformation, ROI and closed loop marketing, rebranding &

repositioning, maker to market strategies, start-up coaching, change management and more...

Feel free to contact Sander Arts at Orange Tulip Consultancy, LLC at: sander1arts@gmail.com

https://www.linkedin.com/in/sander1arts/

Sander is also on Twitter: @Sander1Arts

157

GriDD effective information

GriDD makes information effective for organizations. The GriDD team consists of Information architects that design, create and implement smart information concepts. On the edge of new digital developments and proven business principles, GriDD re-invents professional services by being the one-stop shop for effective information products such as smart portals, websites, applications and content. Offering all the necessary support ranging from concepts, designs and prototypes to strategy and realization support. Whatever it takes.

Whenever organizations have complex challenges or want to create effective experiences for their customers or employees, GriDD brings in world class methodologies and tools to drive change and generate bottom line results.

Feel free to contact GriDD at:
info@gridd.nl

www.gridd.nl/en

ACKNOWLEDGEMENTS

The journey towards this book started a year ago with an email having the following subject line: "We should write a book, maybe!?". The three of us, being colleagues, team mates and, most importantly, friends, thought we'd share our experiences to help others be more effective in business and marketing. So, we went on a journey. Along the way, we learned (and laughed) a lot, met new people and worked with some great minds that have the drive to make marketing work. So many professionals were involved that it is almost undoable to thank them all. But we do want to take a shot at it, since we feel we owe it to them:

The global teams from companies we worked for: NXP team, Atmel team, Philips Lighting team.

The agencies that stretched our (and each other's) abilities: SupplyFrame, Text100, Centagon, Pyramidion, TriMM, Saristos, WideOpenNetworks, NovaSilva, Adaptive Path, Philips Design, McKinsey, DemandBase, Stanford GSB, HackaDay, Hackster.io, SnappApp, Domo, Eloqua, Oracle, DigiKey, Brand50, BellHill, Clock Four, MediaCatalyst, BackBase, Present-Media, SayYeah, SDL, RTB Social, DemandFrontier, Legacy, Publitek, RP Group, Sparks, CG Solutions, Shift Communications, Lucy Turpin and Artie Beavis.

Special thanks go to Han Nabben and Michel Claassens. As Cut the Bullsh*t marketeers *avant la lettre* they explored and pioneered with us towards new ways of marketing to realize true impact in complex and dynamic environments. Having them as Cut the Bullsh*t marketing ambassadors is of great value to us.

We also like to give special thanks to the endorsers of this book: Frans van Houten, Baba Shiv, Johannes P. Huth, Mike Noonen, Rick Clemmer and Steve Laub.

Their leadership and support for what we were doing sometimes consisted of 'tough love'. We are truly humbled by their friendship, guidance, and coaching on the journey we went through from good to great. Their endorsements for this book mean the world to us.

And, last but not least, the professionals that made the book really exceptional: Edith Doosje, Maaike Schutten, Fenna Klein Tuente and Robert Slagter.

Sander Arts, Mark Geljon, Jeroen Grit